lonely planet

NAPLES & THE AMALFI COAST

TOP EXPERIENCES • LOCAL LIFE

CRISTIAN BONETTO
BRENDAN SAINSBURY

Contents

Plan Your Trip 4

COVID-19

We have re-checked every business in this book to ensure that it is still open after the COVID-19 outbreak. However, the economic and social impacts of COVID-19 will continue to be felt long after the outbreak has been contained, and many businesses, services and events referenced in this guide may experience ongoing restrictions. Some businesses may be temporarily closed, have changed their opening hours and services, or require bookings; some unfortunately could have closed permanently. We suggest you check with venues before visiting for the latest information.

Explore Naples & the Amalfi Coast 27

Worth a Trip

Survival Guide 143

Special Features

Left: Pompeii (p92) JAVEN/SHUTTERSTOCK ©

Naples & the Amalfi Coast's Top Experiences

Walk through history at the Museo Archaeologico Nazionale (p52)

JOLANTA WOJCICKA/SHUTTERSTOCK ©

Discover Pompeii (p92)

GIMAS/SHUTTERSTOCK ©

Wander the Palazzo Reale di Capodimonte (p66)

ANBUSIELLO R/ALAMY ©

Explore the Cappella Sansevero (p30)

View treasures at Certosa e Museo di San Martino (p74)

MARCOBRIVIO.PHOTO/SHUTTERSTOCK ©

Marvel at the Reggia di Caserta (p104)

FRANCESCO BONINO/SHUTTERSTOCK ©

MITZO/SHUTTERSTOCK ©

Worship at the Duomo (p32)

Gaze at the Palazzo Reale (p56)

ALEPANA/SHUTTERSTOCK ©

Behold Positano (p122)

ANDREW MAYOVSKYY/SHUTTERSTOCK ©

LUCAMATO/SHUTTERSTOCK ©

Climb in Ravello (p128)

Retreat to the Capri Villas (p108)

ROMAN PLESKY/SHUTTERSTOCK ©

BOUMEN JAPET/SHUTTERSTOCK ©

Uncover Herculaneum (Ercolano; p100)

Dining Out

Dining in Naples and on the Amalfi Coast is a mouth-watering experience. Everything seems to taste that little bit better here – the tomatoes are sweeter, the mozzarella is silkier and the caffè is richer and stronger. In the shadow of Vesuvius, food, identity and pride are inseparable.

Pizza Napoletana

In 2017, Unesco declared Neapolitan wood-fired pizza part of the 'intangible cultural heritage of humanity'. And yet, the city is also famous for *pizza fritta* (fried pizza), a deep-fried, calzone-like concoction traditionally stuffed with *provola* (provolone) cheese, ricotta, *cicoli* (dried lard) and a dash of tomato *sugo* (sauce). Good *pizza fritta* is light and easily digestible, not to mention a cheap lunch staple.

Regional Pasta

Naples' classic pasta dishes include *spaghetti alle vongole,* a simple yet spectacular concoction of spaghetti with clams, garlic, *peperoncino* (red chilli pepper) and fresh parsley. A significantly heartier staple is slow-cooked *pasta alla genovese,* an onion-and-beef sauce commonly paired with *ziti* (a thin, tubular pasta). Its soulmate is *ragù napoletano,* a rich, intense combination of slow-cooked tomato *sugo*, onion and meat that is a Sunday classic.

Sweet Treats

Neapolitans adore *babà,* a rum-soaked sponge cake, and *sfogliatella,* a pastry filled with cinnamon-spiced ricotta. The latter comes in two forms: denser *frolla* (shortbread pastry) and flakier *riccia* (filo pastry). Capri claims *torta caprese,* a flourless almond-and-chocolate torte, while the Amalfi Coast claims *delizia di limone,* a sponge cake filled with lemon cream and *limoncello* (lemon liqueur) and coated in a lemon glaze.

CATHERINAUNGER/GETTY IMAGES ©

Best Pizza

Concettina Ai Tre Santi Slow Food toppings and flawless bases from Naples' current 'It kid'. (p70)

Pizzeria Starita A labyrinthine classic with links to Sophia Loren. (p71)

Pizzeria Gino Sorbillo Domain of celebrity *pizzaiolo* Gino Sorbillo. (p41)

Pizzeria Da Franco Tin trays of flawless, crispy-base pizza in Sorrento. (p138)

Best Seafood

Officina del Mare A less-obvious top choice on Naples' touristy Borgo Marinaro. (p86)

Pescheria Mattiucci Beautiful made-to-order *crudo* (raw seafood) at a Neapolitan fishmonger. (p86)

O'Puledrone A Sorrento spot, where you can catch your own meal. (p137)

Il Geranio Romantic views and superlative seafood specialities on Capri. (p115)

La Cambusa High-quality seafood overlooking Positano's main beach. (p126)

Best for Gourmands

Donna Rosa A historic, family-run restaurant and cooking school above Positano. (p127)

Casa Mele Forward-thinking regional fare plus cooking classes in Positano. (p126)

La Palette Local island produce meets creative prowess on Capri. (www.lapalette.it; ☎081 837 72 83; Via Matermània 36; ⏰11am-midnight; meals from €35)

President An affordable Michelin-starred maverick in Pompeii. (p93)

Best Home-Cooking

Da Ettore Produce-driven Neapolitan cooking in a tiny, soulful, family-run space. (p84)

Antica Osteria Da Tonino Handwritten menus and sixth-generation servers in Naples. (p85)

Osteria della Mattonella Comforting *zuppe* (soups), pasta and more at mamma Antonietta's tile-clad Neapolitan classic. (p61)

C'era Una Volta Affordable, time-tested classics in Positano. (p127)

Bar Open

Although southern Italians aren't big drinkers, Naples and, to a lesser extent, the Amalfi Coast offer an increasingly varied selection of venues in which to imbibe. You'll find well-worn wine bars and a new wave of options focused on craft beer, cocktails and even specialty coffee.

The Art of Caffè

While swilling *caffè* is an integral part of local life, it's usually in the form of a quick swill standing at the bar; Neapolitans down their espresso in three sips or less. When ordering an espresso, ask for *un caffè*. Some places will automatically sugar the coffee, so ask for it *amaro* (without sugar) if you don't want it *zuccherato* (with sugar). Most baristas will offer you a glass of water, either *liscia* (still) or *frizzante* (sparkling), with your espresso. Drink it before your coffee to cleanse your palate. To drink like the locals, keep milky options like *caffè latte* and cappuccino for the morning. For a weaker coffee ask for a *caffè lungo* (a watered-down espresso in a larger cup) or a *caffè americano* (an even weaker version of the *caffè lungo*).

Spirited Locals

Sorrento's lauded *limone di Sorrento* (Sorrento lemon) – known for its extreme juiciness and high levels of essential oils and mineral salts – is used to make *liquore di limone di Sorrento,* the area's premium *limoncello* liqueur. The Amalfi Coast's local lemon, the *limone Costa d'Amalfi,* is also used to make the famous lemon liqueur. Yet, the Amalfi Coast is known for more than *limoncello,* using local mountain herbs and plants to create classic *digestivi* like *finocchietto* (wild-fennel liqueur), *fragolino* (wild-strawberry liqueur) and *nocillo,* a liqueur made with walnuts traditionally harvested on the night of St John (24 June).

JEAN-BERNARD CARILLET/LONELY PLANET ©

Best Coffee

Caffè Gambrinus Sucker-punch espresso in a belle-époque Neapolitan landmark. (pictured; p62)

Ventimetriquadri Single-origin beans and Third-Wave brewing in Naples. (p73)

Campana Campania's first speciality roaster in Pompeii. (www.facebook.com/campanabottega; ☎081 1966 4530; Via Sacra 44; 🕐 7.30am-10.30pm Tue-Fri, to 11.30pm Sat & Sun)

Caffè Mexico Rich brews in a swill-and-go retro icon. (p63)

Best Cocktails

L'Antiquario Impeccable cocktails and a speakeasy vibe in Naples. (p87)

D'Anton Well-crafted cocktails in a Sorrento interior-design store. (p139)

Best Wine

L'Ebbrezza di Noè Intriguing wines and bubbles in a snug wine shop, bar and restaurant in Naples. (p84)

Jamón Well-chosen wines and artisanal bites on a Neapolitan piazza. (p44)

Antica Cantina Sepe Cheap vino sourced straight from the makers in Naples. (p71)

Viva Lo Re An impeccable cellar, plus beautiful bites in Ercolano. (p101)

Bollicine Sample both well-known and smaller producers in Sorrento. (p140)

Best Aperitivi

Barril Free pre-dinner nibbles in a garden-like setting in Naples. (p87)

Cantine Sociali Buzzing Neapolitan crowds and varied buffet bites. (p88)

Best Clubs

Spazio Intolab Creative types and niche DJs in a former Naples convent. (p45)

Taverna Anema e Core A celeb-loved Capri classic. (p117)

Music on the Rocks Top DJs by Positano's main beach. (p123)

Treasure Hunt

Beyond the kitschy corno *(horn-shaped charm) key rings and pizza-themed fridge magnets, Naples and the Amalfi Coast offer a plethora of covetable local buys, reflecting local ingenuity and centuries of sharply tweaked know-how.*

Top Souvenirs

Naples is a hub for artists and creatives, and many are inspired by the city's ancient legends and landscapes. Among them are jewellery designers Asad Ventrella: Contemporastudio (p88) and Mattana Design (p89) and *presepe* (nativity crib) master La Scarabattola (p46). Mt Vesuvius inspires a line of bags at family-owned Scriptura (p46), while the city's world-famous glove-making tradition continues at Omega (p71). Neapolitan style is also on offer at high-end outfitter E. Marinella (p79), famous for its silk ties. Capri is famous for its eponymous pants and historic perfumery Carthusia I Profumi di Capri (p117), while Sorrento is celebrated for its marquetry, gracing everything from jewellery boxes to card tables. The best shops line the narrow streets of Sorrento's *centro storico*, among them Stinga (p141). On the Amalfi Coast, Positano is known for its handmade leather *sandali* (sandals) while the coast itself is also known for its brightly hued ceramics.

Tax-Free Shopping

A 22% value-added tax known as IVA (Imposta sul Valore Aggiunta) is included in the price of most goods and services. Non-EU residents who spend more than €155 at one shop at a single time can claim a refund when leaving the EU. The refund only applies to purchases from stores that display a 'Tax Free' sign. For more information, see www.taxrefund.it.

MAZERATH/SHUTTERSTOCK ©

Best for Local Fashion

E. Marinella Luxe silk ties and niche accessories in Naples. (p79)

Omega Neapolitan leather gloves coveted from Paris to Tokyo. (p71)

Livio De Simone Bold, colour-forward frocks, *robe chemesiers* and more for chic individualists. (p89)

La Parissienne Ready-to-wear and bespoke Capri pants on their namesake island. (p117)

La Bottega di Brunella Pure linen and silk women's threads designed and made in Positano. (p124)

La Botteguccia de Giovanni Handcrafted, made-to-measure leather sandals, also in Positano. (p124)

Best for Beauty

Carthusia I Profumi di Capri Artisan fragrances for women and men from Capri. (pictured; p117)

Kiphy Natural, heavenly scented soaps and beauty products made in-store in Naples. (p47)

Best for Craft & Design

Bottega 21 Cool, locally made bags, wallets, notebook covers and more in Naples and Sorrento. (p45)

MAC Ceramics Whimsical, affordable, handmade ceramic bowls, plates and jewellery in Naples. (p47)

Asad Ventrella: Contemporastudio Sophisticated yet playful unisex jewellery design in Naples. (p88)

La Scarabattola Contemporary ceramic objects inspired by Neapolitan folklore. (p46)

Mattana Design Richly detailed, unisex jewellery made in Naples. (p89)

Stinga Beautifully crafted inlaid-wood objects plus jewellery in Sorrento. (p141)

Talarico Cult-status umbrellas made by a master and his nephew in Naples. (p63)

Best for Food Lovers

Limonè Artisan liqueurs and take-home edibles made with local lemons in Naples' *centro storico*. (p47)

Archaeology

TRABANTOS/SHUTTERSTOCK ©

With almost 3000 candles on its birthday cake, Naples and its sparkling coastline claim some of Italy's most famous and important archaeological sites. From Greek city walls to frescoed Roman villas and catacombs, history here is written large.

The Early Years

The ancient Greeks were the first major players on the scene, setting up a trading post on Ischia and another settlement at Cumae (Cuma) in the 8th century BC. According to legend, the traders also established Naples on the island of Megaris, current home of the Castel dell'Ovo in about 680 BC. Christened Parthenope, its namesake was a suicidal siren. Unable to lure the cunning Ulysses with her songs, she drowned herself, washing up on shore. In 474 BC, the Cumaeans founded Neapolis (New Town) where Naples' *centro storico* (historic centre) now stands. In 421 BC the Greeks fell to the Samnites. They, in turn, proved no match for the Romans, who took Neapolis in 326 BC. The death of the last Roman emperor, Romulus Augustus, in AD 476 saw the city pass into barbarian hands.

Best Archaeological Sites

Pompeii A wonderland of ancient Roman vestiges, from chariot-grooved streets to theatres and temples and a brothel. (p92)

Herculaneum More compact and even better preserved than Pompeii. (p100)

Museo Archeologico Nazionale Naples' incomparable hoard of ancient sculptures, mosaics, frescoes and decorative arts. (p52)

Villa Oplontis The reputed home of Emperor Nero's second wife, adorned with fabulous frescoes. (www.pompeiisites.org; adult/reduced incl Boscoreale €7/4)

Catacombe di San Gennaro Naples' oldest catacombs claim the earliest-known image of San Gennaro. (pictured above; p69)

Villa Jovis Tiberius' clifftop Capri villa offers views fit for the most demanding of emperors. (p109)

Architecture & Art

Millennia of political conquests and struggles, of human ingenuity, creativity and ambition, have bestowed Naples with an architectural and artistic legacy that few corners of Europe can match. It's an overwhelming list, so why not start with the undisputed highlights?

ARKANTO/SHUTTERSTOCK ©

Best Palaces & Villas

Reggia di Caserta Italy's largest royal palace, with stunning gardens that sprawl for kilometres. (pictured above; p104)

Palazzo Reale di Capodimonte Naples' hilltop Bourbon behemoth, with a centuries-spanning art collection that is one of Italy's finest. (p66)

Villa Rufolo A centuries-old Ravello abode famed for its soul-stirring gardens, views and summertime concerts. (p129)

Villa Lysis The former art nouveau Capri hideaway of French poet Jacques d'Adelsward-Fersen, complete with opium den. (p109)

Best Baroque Legacies

Cappella Sansevero Sanmartino's *Cristo velato* is only one of several astounding baroque artworks inside this esoteric Neapolitan chapel. (p30)

Duomo Some of Naples' most illustrious baroque artists contributed to the cathedral's astounding Cappella di San Gennaro. (p32)

Certosa e Museo di San Martino A hilltop Neapolitan monastery with one of Italy's most spectacular baroque churches. (p74)

Palazzo dello Spagnolo Not so much a staircase as an operatic tribute to the Neapolitan spirit. (p69)

Best Modern & Contemporary Art

MADRE Naples' foremost collection of modern and contemporary art. (p39)

Gallerie d'Italia – Palazzo Zevallos Stigliano Beautiful 19th-century landscapes, portraits and sculptures, plus Caravaggio's haunting epilogue. (p59)

Galleria Lia Rumma On-point exhibitions of Italian and foreign artists in the former apartment of a prolific curator and collector. (p83)

Thomas Dane Gallery Another prolific private gallery, with rotating exhibitions of modern art in a crisp, Liberty-style space in Naples. (p83)

Under the Radar

GIAMBATTISTA LAZAZZERA/SHUTTERSTOCK ©

Even in the crowded towns and cities of Italy's most populous region there are ways of escape, places where a spontaneous turn down a narrow backstreet will usher you away from the gelato-seeking hordes and deposit you at the gates of a garden, village or trail that's been long overlooked.

Sentiero dei Fortini

Winding its way along Capri's surprisingly rugged west coast, this blustery trail skirts the ruins of three diminutive forts. It stretches from Punta dell'Arcera near the Grotta Azzurra to Punta Carena at the island's southwestern tip.

Orto Botanico di Napoli

The perfect antidote to a hot summer's day, these **botanical gardens** (081 253 39 37; www.ortobotanico.unina.it; Via Foria 223; 9am-2pm Mon, Wed & Fri, to 4pm Tue & Thu; 147, 182, 184 to Via Foria) belong to a local university and harbour a collection of plant species from around the globe.

Valle del Sambuco

A little-trodden walking circuit that delves into the hills and valleys behind the twin Amalfi towns of Maiori and Minori. Scented by lemon groves and scattered with ruins, it reaches its lofty climax at a 13th-century convent perched high above the Mediterranean.

Cetara

Cetara is a fiercely traditional fishing village with a reputation as a gastronomic hotspot. Its main catch is anchovies which are made into a distinctive food seasoning called *colatura di alici*.

Atrani

The smallest village in southern Italy by area, Atrani (pictured) is Amalfi town's more hushed, humbler cousin that sits shoehorned into a narrow, steep-sided valley where it's been left to develop in splendid isolation.

For Kids

With a little planning and some background information on the region's gripping history, Naples and the Amalfi Coast are guaranteed to hook young, curious minds. After all, this is the land of giant gladiatorial arenas, mysterious catacombs, hissing craters and bubbling beaches. Jump in!

JACQUELINE F COOPER/SHUTTERSTOCK ©

Children are adored in Naples and welcomed almost anywhere. Most museums and sights offer discounted entry for kids, although some discounts are for EU citizens only. Trattorias and pizzerias are especially welcoming of kids, and though children's menus are uncommon, requesting a *mezzo piatto* (half plate) from the menu items is usually fine.

Ask at tourist offices about any family activities and events, and consider investing in a few children's history books to help their imagination along at archaeological sites. Cobbled streets, pot holes and crowded transport make travelling with a stroller cumbersome; consider investing in an ergonomic baby carrier instead.

Best for Time Travel

Pompeii Ancient theatres, houses, shops, even a stadium. The ancient brothel will no doubt bemuse teens. (p92)

Herculaneum Smaller than Pompeii and better preserved, with carbonised furniture and ancient shop advertisements. (p100)

Napoli Sotterranea Head down a secret porthole into a magical labyrinth of Graeco-Roman passageways and cisterns right below Naples. (p40)

Cimitero delle Fontanelle It's Halloween every day at the ghoulish Fontanelle Cemetery, neatly stacked with human skulls and bones. (p69)

Best for Outdoor Thrills

Grotta Azzurra Pixar has nothing on Capri's dazzling, other-worldly Blue Grotto. (pictured above; p115)

Mt Vesuvius Peer into the crater of mainland Europe's only active volcano. (p98)

Four Perfect Days

Day 1

INU/SHUTTERSTOCK ©

Start with a burst of baroque in the **Chiesa del Gesù Nuovo** (pictured above; p38), clear your mind in the majolica-tiled cloister of the **Complesso Monumentale di Santa Chiara** (p38), then pay tribute to the magnificent *Cristo velato* sculpture inside **Cappella Sansevero** (p30).

After lunch at **Tandem** (p41) or **Salumeria** (p41), lose yourself in ancient mosaics and marble brawn at the blockbuster **Museo Archeologico Nazionale** (p52) or critique contemporary art at **MADRE** (p39). If there's still time, take in the vainglorious **Duomo** (p32) before dinner at **Donna Romita** (p41) or standout pizzeria **Concettina Ai Tre Santi** (p70). For a nightcap, hit the bars on **Piazza Bellini** (p44).

Day 2

TOMASZ WOZNIAK/SHUTTERSTOCK ©

Nibble on a *sfogliatella* from **Sfogliatella Mary** (p61) while detouring through **Galleria Umberto I** (p60) to **Caffè Gambrinus** (p62) for morning espresso. Catch the nearby shuttle bus to **Palazzo Reale di Capodimonte** (p66), a palace crammed with priceless artworks.

After a casual lunch at **Da Luisa** (p67), tour the ancient **Catacombe di San Gennaro** (p69), then scale **Castel dell'Ovo** (pictured above; p82) for a sea-and-city panorama. Rehydrate at lo-fi waterfront bar **Al Barcadero** (p88) before feasting on seafood at **Officina del Mare** (p86). Alternatively, hit trendy Chiaia for *aperitivo* at **Barril** (p87) or **Cantine Sociali** (p88) and dinner at **Dialetti** (p85).

RUI VALE SOUSA/SHUTTERSTOCK ©

On day three, hop on a hydrofoil to fabled Capri. Turn up before the day trippers descend and join the local who's-who brigade at the emblematic square **La Piazzetta**. Leave the surrounding sophisticated strut of shops behind as you head to **Giardini di Augusto** (p114), with flower-filled terraces and some of the best views on the island. Enjoy a lazy lunch at **Il Geranio** (p115) or **È Divino** (p115), then head up to Anacapri for a bewitching chairlift ride to **Monte Solaro** (pictured above). The peak can also be reached on foot; one of many beautiful hikes on Capri.

Back in Naples, call ahead to reserve a table at classic **Da Ettore** (p84) or wine bar **L'Ebbrezza di Noè** (p84).

GIANNIS PAPANIKOS/SHUTTERSTOCK ©

Travel back two millennia on day four at the ruins of **Pompeii** (p92), easily reached from Naples by Circumvesuviana train. Highlights include the **Villa dei Misteri** (p93), home to one of the largest, most impressive wall paintings from ancient times. Lunch at deli-eatery **Melius** or Michelin-starred **President** (p93) before slurping superlative *caffè* at Campania's first specialty-coffee roastery **Campana** (p13).

Wrap things up with an (in season) opera or ballet at Naples' world-famous **Teatro San Carlo** (pictured above; p59) before toasting to your Neapolitan sojourn at cognoscenti cocktail den **L'Antiquario** (p87).

Need to Know

For detailed information, see Survival Guide p143

Language
Italian

Currency
Euro (€)

Visas
Generally not required for stays of up to 90 days (or at all for EU nationals); some nationalities need a Schengen visa.

Money
ATMs at Naples' Capodichino airport and major train stations; widely available in towns and cities. Credit cards accepted in most hotels and restaurants.

Mobile Phones
Local SIM cards can be used in European, Australian and some unlocked US phones. Other phones must be set to roaming.

Time
Central European Time (GMT/UTC plus one hour)

Daily Budget

Budget: Less than €100

Dorm bed: €15–30

Double room in a budget hotel: €50–110

Pizza or pasta lunch/dinner: €15

Bus, metro or funicular ticket: €1.10

Return train ticket to Pompeii: €5.60

Midrange: €100–200

Double room in a midrange hotel: €80–180

Lunch and dinner in a local restaurant: €25–50

Three-day Artecard pass: €21

Return express-train ticket to Pompeii: €11

Top end: More than €200

Double room in a four- or five-star hotel: €150–450

Top restaurant dinner: €50–120

Hydrofoil to Capri: €21.50 (one-way)

Advance Planning

Two months before Book your hotel and any tickets for the Teatro San Carlo.

One month before Book any cooking courses and email the Biblioteca Nazionale to organise access to its ancient papyri.

One to two weeks before Email the Museo delle Arti Sanitarie for an English-language tour of the Farmacia Storica degli Incurabili. Book tickets to the Cappella Sansevero and tables at higher-end restaurants, especially on Capri and the Amalfi Coast in high season.

Arriving in Naples

Most people arrive in Naples by train or plane.

Naples International Airport (Capodichino)

7km northeast of central Naples.

Bus Alibus runs to Napoli Centrale and ferry terminals, 6am to 11.30pm, €5.
Taxi 24hr, €18–25, plus €5 surcharge from airport.

Napoli Centrale

Just east of the *centro storico* (historic centre).

Bus Numerous city routes, roughly 5.30am to 11pm, €1.10.
Metro Two lines reaching various parts of central Naples, 5.30am or 6am to 11.30pm, €1.10–1.30.
Taxi 24hr, €9–15, plus any surcharge.

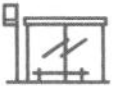

Getting Around

Metro

Line 1 connects Napoli Centrale to Piazza Municipio, Via Toledo and Vomero. Line 2 reaches Chiaia and Mergellina.

Circumvesuviana

Connects Naples to Ercolano (Herculaneum), Pompeii and Sorrento.

Bus

Useful city routes include R4 from Via Toledo to Capodimonte.

Funicular

Three services between central Naples and Vomero (pictured), one between Mergellina and Posillipo.

Taxi

Official taxis are white and metered. Minimum starting fare is €3.50 (€6.50 on Sunday).

Naples & the Amalfi Coast Neighbourhoods

La Sanità & Capodimonte (p65)
Macabre burial sites, baroque staircases and hidden workshops define rough-and-tumble La Sanità, while glorious artworks and gardens await in blue-blooded Capodimonte.

Naples International Airport

Palazzo Reale di Capodimonte

Certosa e Museo di San Martino

Santa Lucia & Chiaia (p77)
The chicest part of town, complete with seafront vistas, high-end shopping, fashionable bars and Naples' oldest castle.

Capri Town & the Isle of Capri (p107)
Chi-chi shopping and dining conspire with ambrosial landscapes, hikes and a spectacular grotto on this celeb-luring island.

Villa San Michele di Axel Munthe

Villa Lysis

Villa Jovis

Reggia di Caserta (15km)

Centro Storico (p29)
Naples' Unesco-lauded historic heart, where soul-stirring art and architecture meet vibrant street life and subterranean ruins.

Herculaneum (Ercolano)

Mt Vesuvius

Toledo & Quartieri Spagnoli (p51)
Home to a glorious theatre, castle and archaeological collection, plus promenading shoppers.

Pompeii

Ravello

Positano

Sorrento & the Amalfi Coast (p121)
A world-famous coastline, famed for its romantic coastal and hilltop towns, glittering waters and superlative seafood.

Explore

Naples & the Amalfi Coast

Worth a Trip

Naples & the Amalfi Coast's Walking Tours

Amalfi, Amalfi Coast (p121) JAVEN/SHUTTERSTOCK ©

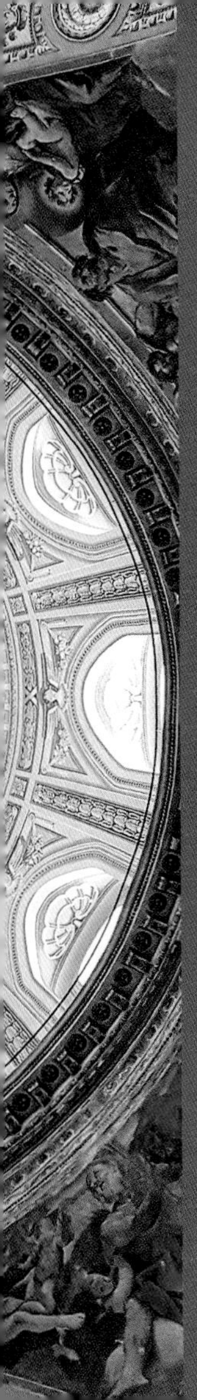

Explore Centro Storico

Naples' World Heritage–listed historic core offers a dizzying rush of bellowing baristas, cultish shrines and operatic palazzi (mansions). The neighbourhood's spectacular cache spans everything from citrus-scented cloisters to frescoed churches, not to mention many of Naples' top eateries, its most boho-spirited bars and its most idiosyncratic artisan studios.

Start with show-stopping artistry at the Chiesa del Gesù Nuovo (p38) and Complesso Monumentale di Santa Chiara (p38). Peer at rare Angevin garments at the nearby Chiesa di San Domenico Maggiore (p38) or head straight to the Cappella Sansevero (p30) for its astounding Cristo velato *sculpture. Lunch on soulful ragù at Tandem (p41) before continuing east to the Duomo (p32), home to a spectacular, fresco-lavished dome. Close by, the Pio Monte della Misericordia (p38) houses an innovative Caravaggio masterpiece. Alternatively, eye up contemporary art at MADRE (p39). Dine on local produce at Salumeria (p41) or Donna Romita (p41), then swill and schmooze on buzzing Piazze Bellini, home to venues including gallery-bar Spazio Nea (p44).*

Getting There & Around

M Dante, Museo, Università and Duomo on Line 1 and Piazza Cavour on Line 2 skirts the *centro storico* (historic centre).

Route R2 runs along Corso Umberto I at the southern end of the neighbourhood, connecting Napoli Centrale to Piazza Trieste e Trento.

Centro Storico Map on p36

Chiesa del Gesù Nuovo (p38) ALEX DEG/SHUTTERSTOCK ©

Top Experience

Explore the Cappella Sansevero

That the Cappella Sansevero is the most visited sight in Naples is hardly surprising. The former stomping ground – and final resting place – of the city's most infamous alchemist lays claim to the Cristo velato *(Veiled Christ), an 18th-century sculpture so extraordinary that many have questioned how only a talented artist's hand could achieve such perfection.*

MAP P36, C4

081 551 84 70

www.museosansevero.it

Via Francesco de Sanctis 19

adult/reduced €7/5

9am-7pm Wed-Mon

M Dante

Cristo velato

Dating from 1753, the chapel's star attraction is Giuseppe Sanmartino's deeply moving depiction of a spent, crucified Christ (pictured). The figure lies under a marble veil so thin that many have wondered whether the chapel's alchemist patron, Prince Raimondo di Sangro, had found a way to transform cloth into stone. Magical or not, the sculpture is an extraordinary work, and one which led the revered neoclassical sculptor Antonio Canova to dramatically declare that he would have given up 10 years of his own life to produce such a masterpiece.

Ceiling Fresco

The Cappella Sansevero is crowned by Francesco Maria Russo's bombastic *Gloria del Paradiso* (Glory of Heaven). Di Sangro was so unimpressed with the fresco that, in his will, he instructed his eldest son to find the best painter to redo the work. Thankfully, his son Vincenzo disobeyed his father's wish and the riotously hued work survives. Somewhat ironically, the prince himself formulated the long-lasting colours used by the artist, which have allowed the fresco to remain intense and untouched since its completion in 1749.

Subterranean Chamber

Beneath the chapel lies di Sangro's secret chamber, home to a pair of meticulously preserved human arterial systems, one of a man, the other of a woman. Rumours have surrounded the figures for centuries. According to one legend, they belonged to di Sangro's hapless servants, murdered for minor disobedience. Not that the prince was a stranger to wild neighbourhood gossip – to many locals, the inventor and Freemason was seen as a local Dr Faustus, a man who had made a pact with the devil to dabble in magic.

★ Top Tip

- Buy your ticket online in advance for fast-track entry into the chapel; it's worth the extra €2 booking fee, especially during peak holiday periods.

Take a Break

- For interesting wines and charcuterie, graze piazza-side at nearby Jamón (p44).
- Lunch or dinner, tuck into flavour-packed Neapolitan *ragù* at Tandem (p41).

Top Experience

Worship at the Duomo

Dedicated to Our Lady of the Assumption and spanning back to the late 13th century, the Duomo is Naples' preeminent religious masterpiece. Its multi-era wonders include Western Europe's oldest baptistery and a magnificent baroque chapel decorated by some of history's most gifted artists. The latter is a fitting home for the relics of Naples' best-loved patron saint, San Gennaro.

MAP P36, E2

Via Duomo 149

cathedral/baptistery free/€2

cathedral 8.30am-1.30pm & 2.30-7.30pm

147, 182, 184 to Via Foria, M Piazza Cavour

Facade

Inspired by the great Gothic cathedrals of central Italy, the cathedral's facade dates from 1905. The lions guarding the main portal, along with the *Madonna and Child* sculpture group in the lunette above it date from the Angevin period. The rest of the main portal's adornments, including the angels and richly decorated spire, as well as the two side portals, date from the early 15th century.

Cappella di San Gennaro

This show-stopping chapel was designed to a Greek-cross plan by Theatine priest and architect Francesco Grimaldi, and completed in 1646. Cosimo Fanzago executed the entrance, statues and inlaid marble decoration, Jusepe de Ribera painted the nail-biting *St Gennaro Escaping the Furnace Unscathed* and Giovanni Lanfranco created the swirling dome fresco, *Paradise*. Hidden behind the altar is a 14th-century silver bust that stores two phials filled with the miraculously liquefying blood of the chapel's eponymous saint.

Basilica & Battistero

Off the left side of the nave is the Basilica di Santa Restituta, founded by Emperor Constantine in the 4th century. The basilica received a radical makeover by architect and scenographer Arcangelo Guglielmelli after an earthquake in 1688. Guglielmelli's theatrical pedigree is clear in the use of volutes, drapery and angels made using stucco and papier-mâché. The painting adorning the volute ceiling is attributed to Luca Giordano. Adjoining the basilica is the 4th-century Battistero di San Giovanni in Fonte, the oldest baptistery in Western Europe. Commissioned by the city's 12th bishop, St Severus, its dome is encrusted with the remains of 4th-century mosaics depicting *Stories of the Testament*.

★ Top Tips

- When planning your visit, consider that the Cappella di San Gennaro has shorter opening hours than the Duomo itself.
- Seek out the Cappella Minutolo (Minutolo Chapel), mentioned in Boccaccio's *Decameron* and considered one of Naples' best-preserved Gothic relics. It's usually open in the morning and late afternoon.

Take a Break

- For cheap, nourishing Neapolitan street food, stop at nearby **Di Matteo** (☎081 45 52 62; www.pizzeriadimatteo.com; Via dei Tribunali 94; snacks from €1, pizzas from €3; ⏰10am-midnight Mon-Sat, 10.30am-3pm Sun; Ⓜ Dante).
- For a classic Neapolitan sit-down lunch or dinner, head further west along Via dei Tribunali to **La Campagnola** (☎081 45 90 34; Via dei Tribunali 47; meals €20-25; ⏰12.30-4pm & 7.30-11.30pm; 📶; Ⓜ Dante).

Walking Tour

A World Heritage Wander

Naples is a city of hidden wonders, legend and contrasts, and no corner of the city illustrates this more than the centro storico. *Thread your way from Port'Alba to the Duomo through a heady, evocative maze where ancient ruins rub shoulders with bohemian bars and boutiques, enigmatic sculptures and frescoes, and the odd secret cloister.*

Walk Facts

Start Port'Alba; M Dante

End Duomo; M Piazza Cavour

Length 1.8km; 2½ hours

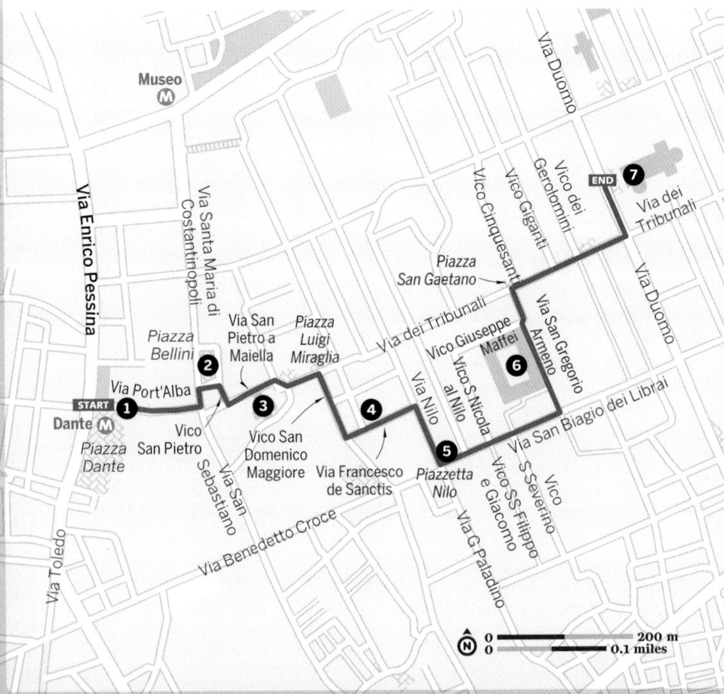

❶ Port'Alba

Start at the old city gate of **Port'Alba**, inaugurated in 1625 by the Spanish viceroy of Naples, Antonio Alvárez. The gate leads into Via Port'Alba, flanked by a handful of bookshops and street-art creations. Turn left into Via Santa Maria di Costantinopoli to reach Piazza Bellini.

❷ Piazza Bellini

The ruins in the middle of bar-flanked **Piazza Bellini** are from the city's 4th-century BC walls, while Palazzo Firrao (Via Santa Maria di Costantinopoli 98) is a particularly beautiful Renaissance-Baroque hybrid.

❸ Chiesa di San Pietro a Maiella

The sounds of strings on Via San Pietro a Maiella emanate from the **Conservatorio di Musica di San Pietro a Majella**, one of Italy's finest music conservatories. To the east is the **Chiesa di San Pietro a Maiella** (☎081 45 90 08; Piazza Luigi Miraglia 25; ⏲8.30am-1pm Mon-Sat, 10-11.30am Sun; Ⓜ Dante), famous for its baroque ceiling paintings, executed by Mattia Preti.

❹ Cappella Sansevero

Close to the church, **Vico San Domenico Maggiore** is dotted with idiosyncratic boutiques and workshops selling local wares. From it, turn left into Via Francesco de Sanctis to view Giuseppe Sanmartino's extraordinary *Cristo velato* sculpture in the **Cappella Sansevero** (p30).

❺ Piazzetta Nilo

This little square claims a river-god statue erected by ancient Alexandrian merchants. The sculpture disappeared when the Egyptian expats moved out, turning up headless in the 15th century. Its restored bearded bonce was added in the 18th century.

❻ Chiesa e Chiostro di San Gregorio Armeno

Located on **Via San Gregorio Armeno** – a street famous for its nativity-crib vendors – the **Chiesa e Chiostro di San Gregorio Armeno** (p40) harbours a tranquil cloister (open mornings only). From the cloister you can enter the beautifully decorated *coro delle monache* (nuns' choir stall), which looks down on the church's baroque nave and altar.

❼ Duomo

Further up the street lies the Gothic simplicity of the **Basilica di San Lorenzo Maggiore**. Take a peek, then turn right into Via Tribunali. At Via Duomo, turn left to reach Naples' spectacular **Duomo** (p32). The cathedral's 17th-century coffered ceiling features paintings depicting *Stories of Christ and the Virgin*, executed by late-mannerist artists including Giovanni Balducci and Giovan Vincenzo Forlì.

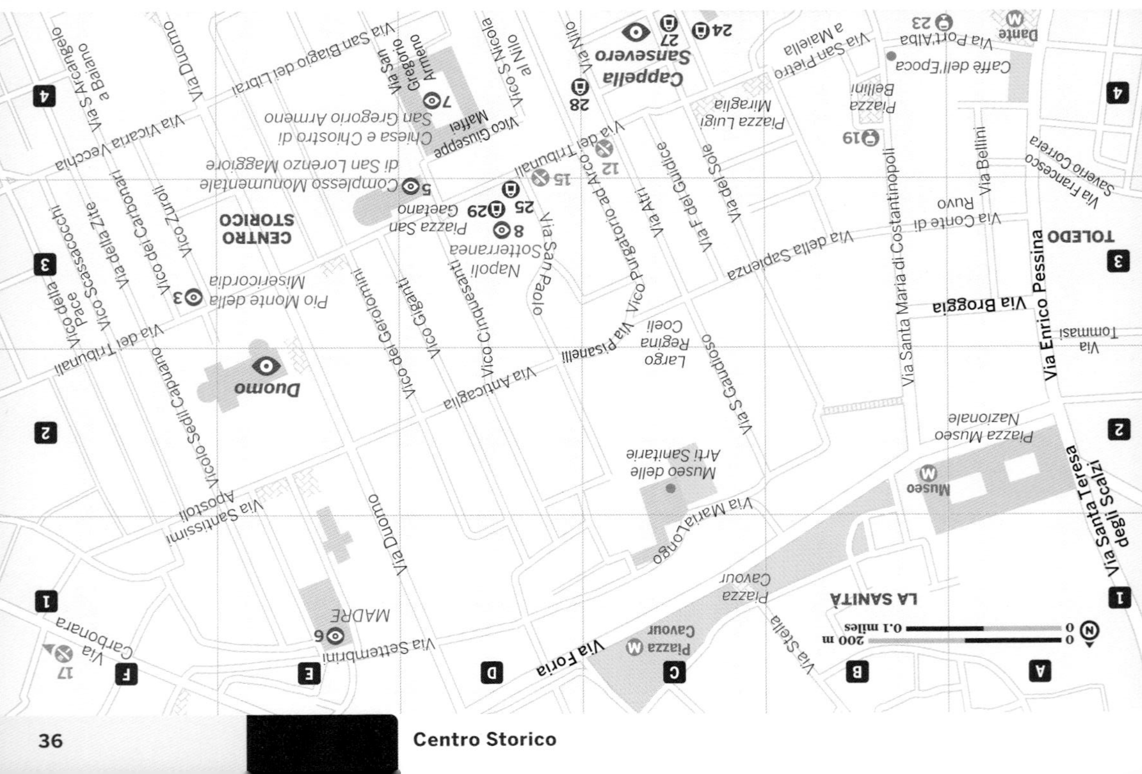

Centro Storico
Duomo
Cappella Sansevero
CENTRO STORICO
LA SANITÀ
TOLEDO
MADRE
Via Foria
Via Duomo
Via dei Tribunali
Via Anticaglia
Via San Paolo
Via Pisanelli
Via Santa Maria di Costantinopoli
Via Enrico Pessina
Via Santa Teresa degli Scalzi
Via Broggia
Via Tommasi
Via Conte di Ruvo
Via Bellini
Via Francesco Saverio Correra
Via Port'Alba
Via San Pietro a Maiella
Via della Sapienza
Via S Gaudioso
Via Atri
Via F del Guidice
Via del Sole
Via Nilo
Vico S Nicola al Nilo
Vico Giuseppe Maffei
Via San Gregorio Armeno
Via San Biagio dei Librai
Via Vicaria Vecchia
Via S Arcangelo a Baiano
Vico della Pace
Vico Scassacocchi
Via della Zite
Vico dei Carbonari
Vico Zuroli
Vicolo Sedil Capuano
Via Santissimi Apostoli
Via Settembrini
Via Carbonara
Via Maria Longo
Via Stella
Vico dei Gerolomini
Vico Giganti
Vico Cinquesanti
Vico Purgatorio ad Arco
Piazza Cavour
Piazza Museo Nazionale
Piazza Bellini
Piazza Luigi Miraglia
Piazza San Gaetano
Largo Regina Coeli
Museo
Dante
Museo delle Arti Sanitarie
Pio Monte della Misericordia
Complesso Monumentale di San Lorenzo Maggiore
Chiesa e Chiostro di San Gregorio Armeno
Napoli Sotterranea
Caffè dell'Epoca
200 m
0.1 miles
A
B
C
D
E
F
1
2
3
4
3
5
6
7
8
12
15
17
19
23
24
25
27
28
29

For reviews see

- Top Experiences p30
- Sights p38
- Eating p41
- Drinking p44
- Shopping p45

A B C D E F
5 6 7 8

DANTE
BORGO OREFICI
Corso Umberto I
Via Nuova Marina
Via Alcide de Gasperi
Via G Sanfelice
Via Monteoliveto
Via Toledo
Via S Anna dei Lombardi
Calata Trinità Maggiore
Via Carrozzieri all Posta
Via Donnalbina
Via S Maria la Nova
Vico Santa Maria dell'Aiuto
Vico Banchi Nuovi
Via Santa Chiara
Complesso Monumentale di Santa Chiara
Via Sedile di Porto
Via S Aspreno
Università
Via A Depretis
Via Marchese Campodisola
Via G C Cortese
Via Porta di Massa
Via Ernesto Capocci
Via S Baldacchini
Via Mezzocannone
Via G Paladino
Vico Donnaromita
Piazzetta del Nilo
Vico SS Filippo e Giacomo
Vico S Severino
Via B Capasso
Via Grande Archivio
Via d'Alagno
Piazza Museo Filangieri
Via dei Cimbri
Duomo
Piazza Nicola Amore
Via Duomo
Vico San Domenico Maggiore
Via Francesco de Sanctis
Chiesa di San Domenico Maggiore
Piazza San Domenico Maggiore
Vico San Geronimo
Via San Giovanni Maggiore Pignatelli
Via S Chiara
Via Pallonetto
Via Benedetto Croce
Via San Sebastiano
Chiesa del Gesù Nuovo
Piazza del Gesù Nuovo
Via Cisterna dell'Olio
Via D Capitelli
Piazza Dante
Piazza Monteoliveto
Via D Lioy
Via T Senise
Via T Caravita
Piazza Carità
Via C Battisti
Piazza Matteotti

1 2 4 9 10 11 13 14 16 18 20 21 22 26

Sights

Complesso Monumentale di Santa Chiara BASILICA

1 MAP P36, B6

Vast, Gothic and cleverly deceptive, the mighty **Basilica di Santa Chiara** stands at the heart of this tranquil monastery complex. The church was severely damaged in WWII: what you see today is a 20th-century recreation of Gagliardo Primario's 14th-century original. Adjoining it are the basilica's **cloisters**, adorned with brightly coloured 17th-century majolica tiles and frescoes. (081 551 66 73; www.monasterodisantachiara.it; Via Santa Chiara 49c; basilica free, Complesso Monumentale adult/reduced €6/4.50; basilica 7.30am-1pm & 4.30-8pm, Complesso Monumentale 9.30am-5.30pm Mon-Sat, 10am-2.30pm Sun; M Dante)

Chiesa del Gesù Nuovo CHURCH

2 MAP P36, B5

The extraordinary Chiesa del Gesù Nuovo is an architectural Kinder Surprise. Its shell is the 15th-century, Giuseppe Valeriani–designed facade of Palazzo Sanseverino, converted to create the 16th-century church. Inside, *piperno*-stone sobriety gives way to an astonishing blast of baroque that could make the Vatican blush: a vainglorious showcase for the work of top-tier artists such as Francesco Solimena, Luca Giordano and Cosimo Fanzago. (081 551 86 13; Piazza del Gesù Nuovo; 7am-1pm & 4-8pm Sun-Wed, 7am-8pm Thu-Sat; M Dante)

Pio Monte della Misericordia CHURCH, MUSEUM

3 MAP P36, F3

The 1st-floor gallery of this octagonal, 17th-century church delivers a satisfying, digestible collection of Renaissance and baroque art, including works by Francesco de Mura, Jusepe de Ribera, Andrea Vaccaro and Paul van Somer. It's also home to contemporary artworks by Italian and foreign artists, each inspired by Caravaggio's masterpiece *Le sette opere di misericordia* (The Seven Acts of Mercy). Considered by many to be the most important painting in Naples, you'll find it above the main altar in the ground-floor chapel. (081 44 69 44; www.piomontedellamisericordia.it; Via dei Tribunali 253; adult/reduced €7/5; 9am-6pm Mon-Sat, to 2.30pm Sun; M Piazza Cavour)

Chiesa di San Domenico Maggiore CHURCH

4 MAP P36, C5

Completed in 1324 on the orders of Charles I of Anjou, this was the royal church of the Angevins. Pietro Cavallini's frescoes in the Cappella Brancaccio are among the few surviving 14th-century remnants. Take the guided tour (in Italian, with an English information sheet) to view the **sacristy**, crowned by a ceiling fresco by

Francesco Solimena and home to the sarcophagi of 45 Aragon princes and other nobles. The tour includes a peek at rare historical garments retrieved from the coffins. (☎333 8638997; www.museosandomenicomaggiore.it; Piazza San Domenico Maggiore 8a; guided tours adult/reduced from €5/4; ⏰10am-6pm; MDante)

Complesso Monumentale di San Lorenzo Maggiore ARCHAEOLOGICAL SITE

5 MAP P36, D3

The **basilica** at this richly layered religious complex is deemed one of Naples' finest medieval buildings. Aside from Ferdinando Sanfelice's facade, the Cappella al Rosario and the Cappellone di Sant'Antonio, its baroque makeover was stripped away last century to reveal its austere, Gothic elegance. Beneath the basilica is a sprawl of extraordinary Graeco-Roman **ruins**, accessible on a one-hour guided tour. (☎081 211 08 60; www.laneapolissotterrata.it; Via dei Tribunali 316; church free, museum & excavations guided tours adult/reduced €10/8; ⏰church 8am-7pm, museum & excavations 9.30am-5.30pm; MDante)

MADRE GALLERY

6 MAP P36, E1

When *Madonna and Child* overload hits, reboot at Naples' museum of modern and contemporary art. In the lobby, French conceptual artist Daniel Buren sets the mood with his playful, mirror-panelled

Complesso Monumentale di San Lorenzo Maggiore

A Magnificent Apothecary

Make sure to email the **Museo delle Arti Sanitarie** (Museum of the History of Medicine & Health; Map p36, C2; 081 44 06 47; www.museoartisanitarie.it; Ospedale degli Incurabili, Via Maria Longo 50; museum €4, 90min museum & pharmacy tours adult/reduced €10/6; museum 9am-5pm Mon & Wed-Sat, to 1pm Sun; M Piazza Cavour, Museo) to book a tour of the adjoining Farmacia Storica degli Incurabili. A rare 18th-century apothecary located beside the museum, it's one of the city's most magnificent baroque treasures. The medical museum runs guided tours on Wednesday, Friday, Saturday and Sunday. If you're already in the area, you can always drop by the museum and try your luck joining the next available tour. English-language tours should be requested two weeks in advance.

installation *Work in Situ*, with other specially commissioned installations from heavyweights like Anish Kapoor, Rebecca Horn and Sol Witt on level one. Level two houses the bulk of MADRE's permanent collection of painting, sculpture, photography and installations from other prolific 20th- and 21st-century artists, designers and architects. (Museo d'Arte Contemporanea Donnaregina; 081 1973 7254; www.madrenapoli.it; Via Settembrini 79; adult/reduced €8/4, Mon free; 10am-7.30pm Mon & Wed-Sat, to 8pm Sun; M Piazza Cavour)

Chiesa e Chiostro di San Gregorio Armeno CHURCH, CLOISTER

7 MAP P36, D4

Overstatement knows no bounds at this richly ornamented 16th-century monastic complex. The church packs a visual punch with its lavish wood and papier-mâché choir stalls, sumptuous altar by Dionisio Lazzari, and Luca Giordano's masterpiece fresco *The Embarkation, Journey and Arrival of the Armenia Nuns with the Relics of St Gregory*. Excess gives way to soothing tranquillity in the picture-perfect cloisters, accessible through the gate on Vico Giuseppe Maffei. (081 420 63 85; Via San Gregorio Armeno 44; 9.30am-noon Mon-Fri, to 1pm Sat & Sun; M Dante)

Napoli Sotterranea ARCHAEOLOGICAL SITE

8 MAP P36, D3

This evocative guided tour leads you 40m below street level to explore Naples' ancient labyrinth of aqueducts, passages and cisterns. (Underground Naples; 081 29 69 44; www.napolisotterranea.org; Piazza San Gaetano 68; adult/reduced €10/8; English tours 10am, noon, 2pm, 4pm & 6pm; M Dante)

Eating

Salumeria

NEAPOLITAN €€

9 MAP P36, C6

Small producers, local ingredients and contemporary takes on provincial Campanian recipes drive bistro-inspired Salumeria. Nibble on quality charcuterie and cheeses or fill up on artisanal *panini* (sandwiches), hamburgers or Salumeria's sublime *ragù napoletano* (pasta served in a rich tomato-and-meat sauce slow-cooked over two days). Even the ketchup here is made in-house, using DOP Piennolo tomatoes from Vesuvius. (081 1936 4649; www.salumeriaupnea.it; Via San Giovanni Maggiore Pignatelli 34/35; panini from €5, charcuterie platters from €8, meals around €30; 12.30-4.30pm & 7.30pm-midnight Mon, Tue, Thu & Sun, 7.30pm-midnight Wed, 7.30pm-12.30am Fri, 12.30-4.30pm & 7.30pm-12.30am Sat; ; M Dante)

Donna Romita

NEAPOLITAN €

10 MAP P36, D5

With a street-level bar and basement dining room, hip, minimalist Donna Romita serves gorgeous, locavore fare with competent modern tweaks. The emphasis is on regional ingredients from smaller producers, whether it's sweet, fragrant Montoro onions or organic olive oil from the Vallo di Diano. Even the wine list is an all-Campanian affair, from the *bollicine* (sparkling wines) to the post-dinner grappa. (081 1851 5074; www.donnaromita.it; Vico Donnaromita 14; cheese & charcuterie platter for 2 €20, meals €20-25; 7pm-1.30am Tue-Thu, to 2am Fri, 12.30-3.30pm & 7pm-2am Sat, 12.30-3.30pm & 7pm-12.30am Sun; ; M Dante)

Tandem

NEAPOLITAN €

11 MAP P36, D5

Ragù might be a Sunday-lunch staple in Naples, but laid-back Tandem serves it up all week long. Whether you're tucking into *rigatoni al ragù* or a *ragù* fondue, expect rich, fragrant, warming goodness that could make your nonna weep. Complete with vegetarian options, it's a small, simple spot with a cult following, so head in early or (on weekends) book. (081 1900 2468; Via G Paladino 51; meals €19; 12.30-3.30pm & 7-11.30pm; ; M Dante)

Pizzeria Gino Sorbillo

PIZZA €

12 MAP P36, C4

Day in, day out, this cult-status pizzeria is besieged by hungry hordes. While debate may rage over whether Gino Sorbillo's pizzas are the best in town, there's no doubt that his giant, wood-fired discs – made using organic flour and tomatoes – will have you licking fingertips and whiskers. Head in super-early or prepare to wait. (081 44 66 43; www.sorbillo.it; Via dei Tribunali 32; pizzas from €3; noon-3.30pm & 7-11.30pm Mon-Sat; ; M Dante)

Pizzeria Gino Sorbillo (p41)

'O Sfizio

NEAPOLITAN €

13 MAP P36, B8

It's not atmosphere that draws fans to humble 'O Sfizio, a bargain-priced takeaway by a traffic-ridden thoroughfare. It's the *parmigiana di melanzana* that's so good that many locals vote it above their own mothers' versions. 'O Sfizio's iteration is simply gorgeous, never oily or heavy yet generously laden with *parmigiano reggiano*, mozzarella and slightly crisp aubergine. (081 1895 8824; Via Santa Maria la Nova 50; panini €3.50-5, dishes €4-5; 7am-7pm Mon-Sat; R4 to Via Monteoliveto, M Università, Toledo)

Gay-Odin

SWEETS, GELATERIA €

14 MAP P36, B5

Not so much a chocolatier as an institution, Gay-Odin concocts some of the city's finest cocoa creations, including oh-so-Neapolitan chocolate *'cozze'* (mussels). For a punch to the palate, try the chocolate-coated coffee beans or the fiery *peperoncino-cioccolato* (chilli-chocolate) combo. This branch also sells Gay-Odin's sublime ice cream; the non-sorbet flavours are especially good. (081 551 07 94; www.gay-odin.it; Via Benedetto Croce 61; gelato from €1.70; 9.30am-8pm Mon-Sat, from 10am Sun; M Dante)

Serafino

SICILIAN €

15 MAP P36, D4

A veritable porthole to Sicily, this takeaway stand peddles authentic island street food. Savoury bites include various types of *arancini* (deep-fried rice balls), among them *al ragù* (with meat sauce) and *alla Norma* (with fried aubergine and ricotta). The real reason to head here, however, is for the crisp, flawless cannoli, filled fresh with silky Sicilian ricotta and sprinkled with pistachio crumbs. Bliss. (081 557 14 33; Via dei Tribunali 44; arancini & cannoli €2.50; 11.30am-10pm)

Trattoria Mangia e Bevi

NEAPOLITAN €

16 MAP P36, C7

Gigi Grasso's loud and lively Eat & Drink sees everyone from pierced students to bespectacled *professori* squeeze around the communal tables for delicious home cooking at rock-bottom prices. Scan the daily-changing menu, jot down your choices and prepare yourself for classic hits like grilled *provola* (provolone), earthy *salsiccia* (pork sausage) and *peperoncino*-spiked *friarielli* (local broccoli). (081 552 95 46; Via Sedile di Porto 92; meals €7; 12.30-3.30pm Mon-Fri; ; M Università)

Attanasio

BAKERY €

17 MAP P36, F1

Bite into the piping-hot *sfogliatella* ricotta filling at this retro pastry peddler and discover crispy perfection. But why stop there with so many trays of treats, from creamy *cannolli siciliani* to a runny, rummy *babà*? Savoury fiends shouldn't

Neapolitan Shrines

It only takes a stroll through the *centro storico* to work out that small shrines are a big hit in Naples. A kitschy combo of electric votive candles, Catholic iconography and fresh or plastic flowers, they adorn everything from *palazzo* facades to courtyards and staircases. Most come with an inscription, confirming the shrine as a tribute *per grazie ricevute* (for graces received) or *ex-voto* (in fulfilment of a vow).

Their popularity can be traced back to the days of Dominican friar Gregorio Maria Rocco (1700–82). Determined to make Naples' dark, crime-ridden laneways safer, he convinced the Bourbon monarch to light them up with oil lamps. The lamps were promptly trashed by the city's petty thieves, who relied on darkness to trip up their victims with rope. Thankfully, the quick-thinking friar had a better idea. Banking on the city's respect for its saints, he encouraged locals to erect illuminated shrines. The idea worked and the streets became safer, for even the toughest of petty thieves wouldn't dare upset a celestial idol.

pass up the hearty *pasticcino rustico*, stuffed with *provola*, ricotta and salami. (☎081 28 56 75; Vico Ferrovia 1-4; sfogliatelle €1.30; ⏰6.30am-7.30pm Tue-Sun; Ⓜ Garibaldi)

Drinking

Jamón

WINE BAR

18 MAP P36, C5

Great for a piazza-side graze, this savvy little deli and wine bar sits at the top of sweeping Piazza San Domenico Maggiore. Offerings include niche and harder-to-find charcuterie and cheese; think cinnamon-seasoned Tuscan mortadella and *prosciutto di suino nero dei Nebroli* (Sicily's answer to Spanish *pata negra*). Savour them in a tasting plate, or sliced and freshly stuffed into a crusty *panino*. (☎081 420 24 58; Piazza San Domenico Maggiore 9; panini €5, cheese & charcuterie tasting plates €5; ⏰10am-midnight; Ⓜ Dante)

Cheap Drinks on Piazza Bellini

Locals don't hit **Caffè dell'Epoca** (Map p36, B4; Via Santa Maria di Costantinopoli; ⏰7am-2am Mon-Sat, to 2pm Sun; 📶; Ⓜ Dante) for the drab decor and sallow lighting, but for Piazza Bellini's hottest bargains: €1.50 bottles of Peroni and €2 spritz. These cut-priced libations draw no shortage of art- and music-school students and staffers, who spill out onto the street for fun, boisterous evening sessions. Bantering owner Peppe will even let you bring in a takeaway pizza.

Spazio Nea

CAFE

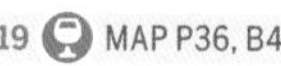

Aptly skirting bohemian Piazza Bellini, this whitewashed gallery features its own cafe-bar speckled with books, flowers, cultured crowds and alfresco seating at the bottom of a baroque staircase. Eye up exhibitions of contemporary Italian and foreign art, then kick back with a *caffé* or a *spritz*. Check Nea's Facebook page for upcoming readings, live music gigs or DJ sets. (☎081 45 13 58; www.spazionea.it; Via Constantinopoli 53; ⏰9am-2am, to 3am Fri & Sat; 📶; Ⓜ Dante)

Palazzo Venezia Napoli

CAFE

This richly historic *palazzo* was gifted to the Venetian Republic in the 15th century as a base for its envoys. The building's 1st floor now houses a small cafe, with a scattering of tables and chairs in a tranquil secret garden. Wind down with a herbal tea or an *aperitivo spritz* surrounded by irises, citrus trees, palms and ferns. (☎081 552 87 39; www.palazzoveneziananapoli.com; Via Benedetto Croce 19; ⏰10am-1.30pm & 3.30-7pm Mon-Sat; Dante)

Shanti Art Musik Bar

BAR

21 MAP P36, D5

Under Tibetan prayer flags, shabby Shanti draws a cosmopolitan crowd of arty and indie types, both local and foreign. While the place serves lunchtime grub, head here in the evenings, when party people congregate at upcycled, candlelit tables to chat, flirt and party well into the night. Drinks are well priced and there's live jazz, blues or soul on Thursday nights. (081 1852 5911; www.facebook.com/shantispaccaNapoli; Via Giovanni Paladino 56; 10am-2am Mon-Wed, to 3pm Thu-Sat; ; M Dante)

Superfly

BAR

22 MAP P36, A5

They may be a little older, but the '90s kids are still partying at this tiny veteran bar, tucked away on a *centro storico* side street. Here, well-mixed drinks, old-school tunes and a fun, easy vibe make it a hit with artists, radicals and middle-class peeps, who spill onto the street, chatting and making the odd new friend. (081 551 03 88; www.facebook.com/soulbar.superfly; Via Cisterna dell'Olio 12; 7pm-1.30am Mon, Wed, Thu & Sun, to 3am Fri & Sat; M Dante)

Libreria Berisio

BAR

23 MAP P36, B4

This midcentury bookshop doubles as buzzing cocktail bar, its wine-red interiors drawing a predominantly young, international crowd. Sip a well-crafted negroni while browsing the floor-to-ceiling bookshelves...or the cute peeps in the crowd. (081 549 90 90; www.facebook.com/berisio; Via Port'Alba 28-29; 9.30am-1.30am Mon-Thu, to 3am Fri, 9.30am-1.30pm & 7pm-3.30am Sat, 6.30pm-1.30am Sun; ; M Dante)

Party in a Cloister

Housed on the 1st floor of the Lanificio – a Bourbon-era wool factory and 15th-century cloister turned culture hub – **Spazio Intolab** (333 9126318; www.facebook.com/intolab; Piazza Enrico De Nicola 46; cover €5-15; 9.30pm-4am Fri & Sat; ; M Garibaldi) draws an easy, arty, cosmopolitan crowd with its all-night parties. Regular DJ sets include in-the-know names from Italy and abroad, playing anything from deep house and techno to live electronica. Check the venue's Facebook page for upcoming events.

Shopping

Bottega 21

FASHION & ACCESSORIES

24 MAP P36, C4

Top-notch Tuscan leather and traditional, handcrafted methods translate into coveted, contemporary leather goods at Bottega 21. Block colours and clean, simple designs underline the range, which includes stylish totes, handbags, backpacks and duffel bags, as well as wallets and coin purses, unisex belts, tobacco pouches and, occasionally, notebook covers. (081 033 55 42; www.bottegaventuno.it; Vico San Domenico Maggiore 21; 9.30am-8pm Mon-Sat)

La Scarabattola ARTS & CRAFTS

25 MAP P36, D3

Not only do La Scarabattola's handmade sculptures of *magi* (wise men), devils and Neapolitan folk figures constitute Jerusalem's official Christmas crèche, but the artisanal studio's fans also include fashion designer Stefano Gabbana and Spanish royalty. Figurines aside, sleek ceramic creations (like Pulcinella-inspired place-card holders) inject Neapolitan folklore with refreshing contemporary style. (081 29 17 35; www.lascarabattola.it; Via dei Tribunali 50; 10.30am-2pm & 3.30-7.30pm Mon-Fri, 10am-8pm Sat; M Dante)

Scriptura FASHION & ACCESSORIES

26 MAP P36, B5

Family-run Scriptura is a must for artisanal leather goods made using high-quality Campanian leather. Its range includes handbags, satchels, duffel bags and backpacks, as well as belts, men's and women's gloves, jackets, wallets, tobacco pouches, eyeglass cases and leather-bound notebooks. Styles and colours cover both the classic and the contemporary and, best of all, prices are reasonable given the quality. (081 552 66 69; Via San Sebastiano 45; 10am-8pm Mon-Sat; M Dante)

Bottles of *limoncello* (lemon liqueur)

Kiphy

COSMETICS

27 MAP P36, C4

In her heavenly scented workshop, Pina Malinconico crafts handmade slabs of soap that look as beautiful as they smell. Lined up under low-slung lights, varieties include a refreshing orange-and-cinnamon blend. The freshly made shampoos, creams and oils use organic, fair-trade ingredients and can be personally tailored. Best of all, products are gorgeously packaged, reasonably priced and made with love. (340 2849691; www.kiphy.it; Vico San Domenico Maggiore 3; 10.30am-2pm & 4-7.30pm Mon-Sat; M Dante)

MAC Ceramics

CERAMICS

28 MAP P36, D4

MAC sells playful, contemporary ceramics created by talented local couple Antimo De Santis and Marina Pascali. Everything is handmade from scratch, from the cube-shaped, pastel-hued necklaces to the polka-dot espresso cups and textile-imprinted dishes. Prices are reasonable, ranging from around €10 for an espresso cup and saucer to around €35 for a teapot. (333 6031376; www.facebook.com/bottegadiceramica; Via Nilo 12; 10am-7pm Mon-Sat; M Dante)

Limonè

FOOD & DRINKS

29 MAP P36, D3

For a take-home taste of Napoli, stock up on a few bottles of Limonè's homemade *limoncello* (lemon liqueur), made with organic lemons from the Campi Flegrei. For something a little sweeter, opt for the *crema di limone,* a gorgeous lemon liqueur made with milk. Other take-home treats include lemon pasta and risotto, lemon-infused chocolate, jars of rum-soaked *babà,* even lemon-infused grappa. (081 29 94 29; www.limoncellodinapoli.it; Piazza San Gaetano 72; 11am-8.30pm; M Dante)

Walking Tour

Mercato & Borgo Orefici

The area wedged between Corso Umberto I and the port is usually overlooked by visitors, yet its labyrinth of ancient streets hides intriguing traditions, myths and street life. Dive in for an atmospheric blend of souk-like market stalls, legend-laced churches, and heirloom businesses peddling everything from jewellery to coveted fabrics.

Getting There

R2 to Corso Umberto I

M Garibaldi

❶ Mercato di Porta Nolana

The **Mercato di Porta Nolana** (Porta Nolana; 8am-6pm Mon-Sat, to 2pm Sun) is Naples at its most *popolana* (working class). Market vendors line gritty streets, peddling fish, vegetables, cheeses and more. The stalls east of the 5th-century Porta Nolana gate stock fashion-label fakes and usually close around 2pm.

❷ Chiesa di Santa Maria del Carmine

This **Chiesa di Santa Maria del Carmine** (081 20 11 96; Piazza del Carmine; 6.30am-12.30pm & 4.30-7.30pm Mon-Sat, 6.30am-12.30pm & 5.30-7.30pm Sun) is the hub for July's Festa della Madonna del Carmine, when fireworks mimic the blaze of the *campanile* (bell tower), reputedly extinguished by the Madonna della Bruna. A 13th-century Byzantine icon of the heavenly firefighter is in the church's 16th-century tabernacle.

❸ Chiesa di Sant'Eligio Maggiore

The stone heads adorning the arch that adjoins the 13th-century **Chiesa di Sant'Eligio Maggiore** (389 5068793; Via Sant'Eligio; 9am-2.30pm Mon-Fri, to 1.30pm Sat) reputedly represent Duke Antonello Caracciolo and maiden Irene Malarbi, the latter forced to sleep with Caracciolo to free her wrongfully imprisoned father. As punishment, Isabella of Aragon forced the duke to marry Malarbi before having him executed.

❹ Chiesa di San Giovanni a Mare

Romanesque **Chiesa di San Giovanni a Mare** (081 26 47 52; Via San Giovanni a Mare 9; 9am-1.30pm) holds a copy of the Donna Marianna, an ancient Greek bust found nearby and once housed there. Its shape inspired the Neapolitan saying "*Me pare Donna Marianna, 'a cap' 'e Napule*", which describes an unattractive woman with a large head.

❺ Fratelli D'Angelo di Donato

Located in Naples' Garment District, family-run **Fratelli D'Angelo di Donato** (081 20 04 87; Via Renovella 5-9; 9am-1pm & 3-7pm Mon-Fri, 9am-1pm Sat) is a go-to for Neapolitan tailors and brides-to-be. In business since 1931, its shelves are a library of fabrics, from prestigious Taroni silk from northern Italy to collectable vintage fabrics from Versace.

❻ Piazzetta Orefici

The labyrinthine streets of the Borgo Orefici have housed Naples' most important goldsmiths, silversmiths and jewellers since medieval times. Its **Piazzetta Orefici** is where the four Consuls of the Goldsmiths' Guild supervised the district's craftsmen.

Explore Toledo & Quartieri Spagnoli

Constructed by Spanish viceroy Pedro Álvarez de Toledo y Zúñiga in the 16th century, Via Toledo (aka Via Roma) heaves with window-shopping teens and elegant palazzi *(mansions). To the south are the glories of Palazzo Reale (p56) and Teatro San Carlo (p59), while to the west, side streets lead into the Quartieri Spagnoli, an earthy warren of dripping washing and renegade Vespas.*

The must-see cultural attractions here are either on (or off) Via Toledo and Piazza Trieste e Trento. Give yourself at least 90 minutes to explore Palazzo Reale (p56) or, for a less taxing morning, admire Caravaggio's swansong at the Gallerie d'Italia – Palazzo Zevallos Stigliano (p59). To the north are the market stalls of La Pignasecca (p60), as well as lunchtime favourite Antica Pizzeria e Trattoria al '22 (p61). Fed, descend into the spectacular Toledo metro station (p60) and head north to the blockbuster Museo Archeologico Nazionale (p52), which merits an entire afternoon of your time.

Getting There & Around

M Line 1 runs north–south through the area. Toledo station is convenient for the Quartieri Spagnoli; Municipio station is best for Castel Nuovo, Palazzo Reale and Teatro San Carlo.

Route R4 runs north along Via Toledo to the Catacombe di San Gennaro and Capodimonte.

Funicolare Centrale and Funicolare di Montesanto run up to Vomero.

Toledo & Quartieri Spagnoli Map on p58

Teatro San Carlo (p59) GIANNIS PAPANIKOS/SHUTTERSTOCK ©

Top Experience

Walk Through History at the Museo Archeologico Nazionale

The stuff history dreams are made of, Naples' Museo Archeologico Nazionale houses one of the world's most important collections of ancient treasures. Its assets include many of the finest frescoes, mosaics and epigraphs from ill-fated Pompeii and Herculaneum, not to mention the largest single sculpture from antiquity unearthed to date, the epic Toro Farnese (Farnese Bull).

MAP P58, C1

081 442 23 28

www.museoarcheologiconapoli.it

Piazza Museo Nazionale 19

adult/reduced €12/6

9am-7.30pm Wed-Mon

Museo, Piazza Cavour

Toro Farnese & Ercole

The undisputed star of the ground-floor Farnese collection of colossal Greek and Roman sculptures is the *Toro Farnese* (Farnese Bull). Mentioned in the *Natural History* of Pliny the Elder, the early 3rd-century masterpiece – most likely a Roman copy of a Greek original – is the largest single sculpture recovered from antiquity. Unearthed in Rome in 1545, the piece was restored by Michelangelo before being escorted to Naples by warship in 1788. Sculpted from a single block of marble, the masterpiece depicts the humiliating demise of Dirce, Queen of Thebes, tied to a raging bull and violently dragged to her death. Directly opposite the work is mighty *Ercole* (Hercules), also discovered at Rome's Baths of Caracalla, albeit without his legs. Michelangelo commissioned Guglielmo della Porta to sculpt replacement pins. The original legs were later uncovered and reinstated by the Bourbons. An inscription on the rock below Hercules' club attributes the work to Athenian sculptor Glykon.

Mezzanine Mosaics & Erotica

The museum's mezzanine level is awash with precious mosaic panels, most of which hail from ancient Pompeii. Room LIX is home to the playful *Scena di commedia: musici ambulanti*, depicting four roaming musicians, as well as the allegorical *Memento mori*, in which a skull represents death, a butterfly the soul, and the wheel fate. The mosaics in rooms LX and LXI are even more impressive. Once adorning the largest home in Pompeii, the Casa del Fauno, they include an action-packed mural of Alexander the Great in battle against Persian king Darius III. Considered one of the most important works of art from antiquity, it's a precise copy of a famous Hellenistic painting from the second half of the 4th century BC. The mosaics found in the Casa del Fauno were created by

★ Top Tips

- Consider buying the *National Archaeological Museum of Naples* (€12), published by Electa; if you want to concentrate on the highlights, audio guides (€5) are available in English.
- To avoid museum burnout, start with the *Toro Farnese* and *Ercole*, explore the mezzanine level and then focus on the 1st-floor frescoes and Villa dei Papiri sculptures. If you still have energy, hit the basement epigraphs and Egyptian relics.

✕ Take a Break

- Tuck into smashing wood-fired pizzas at nearby hot spot Concettina Ai Tre Santi (p70).
- For an early-evening vino and charcuterie session, **La Stanza del Gusto** (☎081 40 15 78; www.lastanzadelgusto.com; Via Costantinopoli 100; platters €10-20, tasting menus €35-65; ⏰5.30pm-midnight Mon, 11am-midnight Tue-Sat; Ⓜ Dante) is a short walk away.

lauded craftsmen from Alexandria, Egypt, active in Italy between the end of the 2nd century BC and the beginning of the 1st century BC. The mezzanine is also home to the Gabinetto Segreto (Secret Chamber), a small, once-scandalous collection of erotically themed artworks and objects. Its most famous piece is a marble sculpture of the mythical half-goat, half-man Pan copulating with a nanny goat.

First-Floor Frescoes & Sculptures

The 1st floor is a tour de force of ancient frescoes, pottery, glassware and sculpture. Room LXXII is home to the largest known depiction of Perseus and Andromeda, in which the hero rescues his young bride after slaying a sea monster. More beast slaying occurs in Room LXXIII, home to a notable depiction of *Theseus the Liberator*. In Room LXXV, *Bacchus and Vesuvius* is believed to represent Vesuvius as it looked before the eruption of 79 AD, with one summit instead of two. A notorious clash between rival spectators at Pompeii's amphitheatre in 59 AD is captured in Room LXXVIII's *Riot between Pompeians and Nucerians*. At the other end of the building, Room CXVI houses the five bronzes known collectively as the *Daughters of Danaus*. Dating from the Augustan period (27 BC–14 AD), the figures represents mythical siblings condemned to pouring water for eternity after murdering their cousins (and bridegrooms) to appease their father, who sought revenge on his own sibling, Aegyptus.

Roman sarcophagus

Museo Archeologico Nazionale

SECOND FLOOR

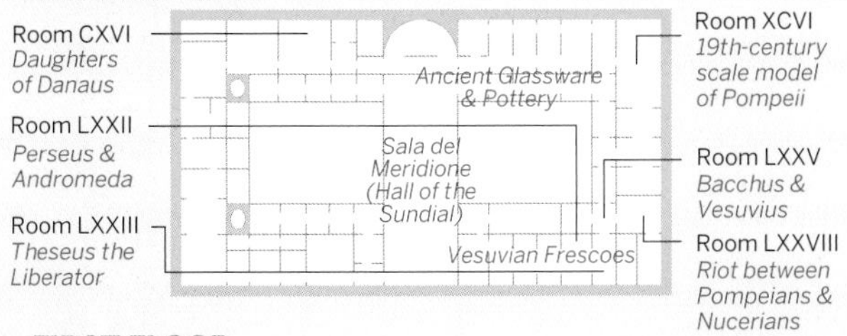

FIRST FLOOR

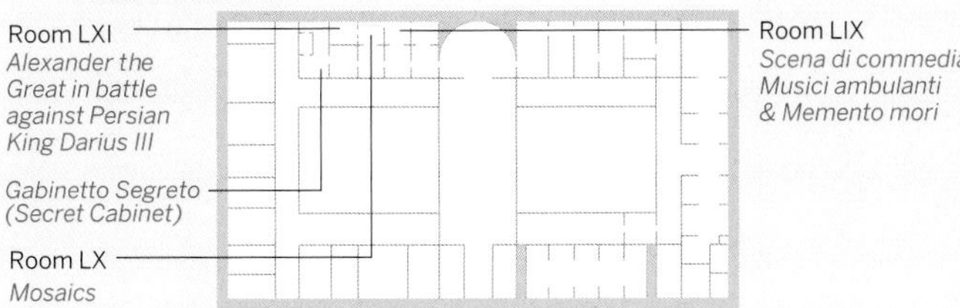

GROUND FLOOR

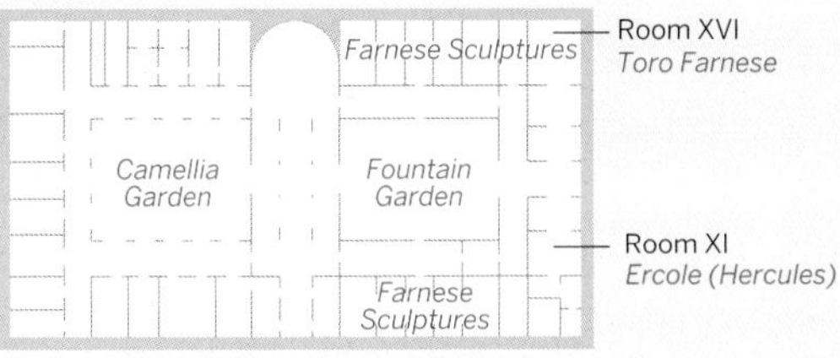

BASEMENT

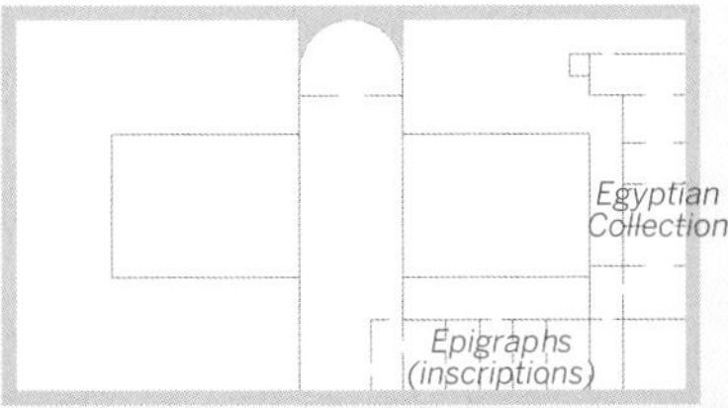

Top Experience

Gaze at the Palazzo Reale

Of the four palaces used by the Bourbons during their rule of the Kingdom of Naples, the Palazzo Reale is the oldest. Conceived by Ferdinando Ruiz de Castro, the Spanish viceroy in Naples between 1599 and 1603, as a suitable pad for Spain's King Phillip III, it remains one of the city's most spectacular, artistically well-endowed pads.

MAP P58, C6

Royal Palace

www.coopculture.it

Piazza del Plebiscito 1

adult/reduced €6/3

9am-8pm Thu-Tue

R2 to Via San Carlo, M Municipio

Architectural Details

The palace was originally designed by late-Renaissance architect Domenico Fontana, with the oldest facade facing Piazza del Plebiscito. The niches along the lower level hold statues of former rulers. Posing from left to right are Roger II of Sicily, Frederick II of Swabia, Charles of Anjou, Alfonso of Aragon, Charles V, Charles III of Bourbon, Joachim Murat and Victor Emmanuel II.

Lavish Interiors & Artworks

The Teatrino di Corte, a private theatre created by Ferdinando Fuga in 1768, makes for an enchanting introduction, with other highlights including late-baroque artist Francesco De Mura's ceiling fresco in Room II and his canvas *Adoration of Shepherds* in Room IV. Remnants from the palace's original decorations include the ceiling-panel paintings by mannerist artist Belisario Corenzio in Room VIII. Room XXIII harbours Queen Maria Carolina's 18th-century rotating reading desk, while the Royal Chapel houses an 18th-century *presepe napoletano* (Neapolitan nativity scene) contributed to by Giuseppe Sanmartino, creator of the *Cristo velato* sculpture in Naples' Cappella Sansevero.

Biblioteca Nazionale

Italy's third-largest library occupies the palace's east wing. Opened by Ferdinand IV in 1804 as the Royal Library of Naples, its vaulted main Reading Room is breathtaking. You'll find a 17th-century globe in the library's Executive Offices section, and extraordinary carved-timber interiors in the Biblioteca Lucchesi Palli (Lucchesi Palli Library) on the 2nd floor. Email the library a month ahead to view its ancient papyri, retrieved from Herculaneum.

★ Top Tips

- Theatre and opera fans can buy the combination ticket (€12) for entry to both the Palazzo Reale and adjoining MeMus (p59) theatre museum.
- Check the Teatro San Carlo website (www.teatrosancarlo.it) for upcoming productions in the Palazzo Reale's Teatro del Cortile.

Take a Break

- For coffee and a cult-status chocolate medallion, head to **Scaturchio** (Teatro San Carlo, Piazza Trieste e Trento; 8am-9.30pm; R2 to Via San Carlo, M Municipio) in neighbouring Teatro San Carlo.
- Savour regional home-cooking at snug **Trattoria San Ferdinando** (081 42 19 64; Via Nardones 117; meals €25-35; 12.30-3.30pm Mon-Sat, 7.30-11pm Tue-Fri; R2 to Via San Carlo, M Municipio), off Piazza Trieste e Trento.

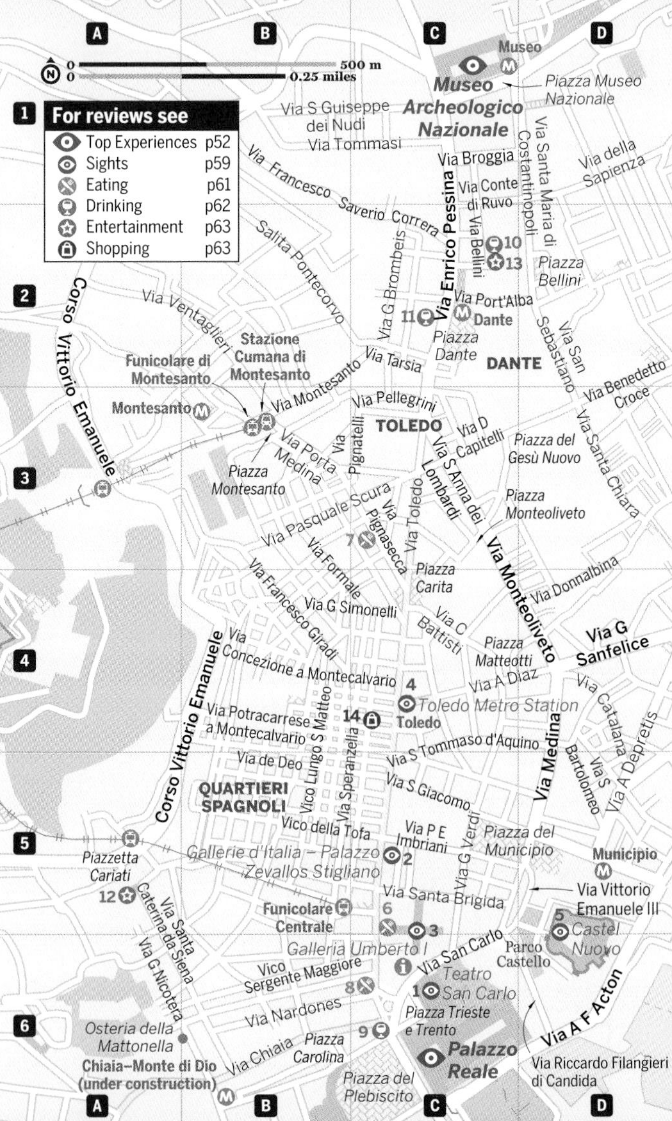

A
B
C
D
1
2
3
4
5
6
0 500 m
0 0.25 miles
For reviews see
Top Experiences p52
Sights p59
Eating p61
Drinking p62
Entertainment p63
Shopping p63
Museo
Museo Archeologico Nazionale
Piazza Museo Nazionale
Via S Guiseppe dei Nudi
Via Tommasi
Via Broggia
Via Santa Maria di Costantinopoli
Via della Sapienza
Via Francesco Saverio Correra
Via Conte di Ruvo
Via Bellini
Via Enrico Pessina
10
13
Piazza Bellini
Salita Pontecorvo
Via G Brombeis
Via Port'Alba
Dante
11
Piazza Dante
Via Ventaglieri
Corso Vittorio Emanuele
Stazione Cumana di Montesanto
Funicolare di Montesanto
Via Tarsia
DANTE
Via San Sebastiano
Via Benedetto Croce
Via Montesanto
Montesanto
Via Pellegrini
TOLEDO
Via D Capitelli
Piazza del Gesù Nuovo
Via Santa Chiara
Via Porta Medina
Via Pignatelli
Via S Anna dei Lombardi
Piazza Montesanto
Via Pasquale Scura
Via Toledo
Piazza Monteoliveto
Via Pignasecca
7
Via Monteoliveto
Via Formale
Piazza Carita
Via Donnalbina
Via Francesco Giradi
Via G Simonelli
Via C Battisti
Via G Sanfelice
Via Concezione a Montecalvario
Piazza Matteotti
Via A Diaz
4
Toledo Metro Station
Via Catalana
Via A Depretis
Via Potracarrese a Montecalvario
14
Toledo
Vico Lungo S Matteo
Via Speranzella
Via S Tommaso d'Aquino
Via de Deo
Via S Bartolomeo
Via Medina
QUARTIERI SPAGNOLI
Via S Giacomo
Vico della Tofa
Via P E Imbriani
Via G Verdi
Piazza del Municipio
Piazzetta Cariati
Gallerie d'Italia – Palazzo Zevallos Stigliano
2
Municipio
Via Vittorio Emanuele III
12
Via Santa Caterina da Siena
Via Santa Brigida
Funicolare Centrale
6
3
5
Castel Nuovo
Galleria Umberto I
Via San Carlo
Parco Castello
Via G Nicotera
Vico Sergente Maggiore
Teatro San Carlo
8
1
Via Nardones
Piazza Trieste e Trento
Via A F Acton
Osteria della Mattonella
9
Via Chiaia
Piazza Carolina
Palazzo Reale
Chiaia–Monte di Dio (under construction)
Piazza del Plebiscito
Via Riccardo Filangieri di Candida

Sights

Teatro San Carlo THEATRE

1 MAP P58, C6

An evening at Italy's largest opera house is magical. Although the original 1737 theatre burnt down in 1816, Antonio Niccolini's 19th-century reconstruction is pure Old World opulence. If you can't make it to a performance, consider taking one of the 45-minute guided tours of the venue. Tours usually take in the foyers, elegant main hall and royal box (the best seat in the house) and tour tickets can be purchased at the theatre up to 15 minutes before each tour begins.

Next door, the Palazzo Reale is home to **MeMus** (Museum & Historical Archive of the Teatro San Carlo; www.memus.squarespace.com; Piazza del Plebiscito; adult/reduced €6/5; 9am-7pm Mon, Tue & Thu-Sat, to 3pm Sun), the theatre's museum. (081 797 24 68; www.teatrosancarlo.it; Via San Carlo 98; guided tours adult/reduced €7/5; guided tours 10.30am, 11.30am, 12.30pm, 2.30pm, 3.30pm & 4.30pm; R2 to Via San Carlo, M Municipio)

Gallerie d'Italia – Palazzo Zevallos Stigliano GALLERY

2 MAP P58, C5

Built for a Spanish merchant in the 17th century and reconfigured in belle-époque style by architect Luigi Platania in the early 20th century, Palazzo Zevallos Stigliano houses a compact yet stunning collection of Neapolitan and Italian

Gallerie d'Italia – Palazzo Zevallos Stigliano

La Pignasecca Market

Mouth-watering **La Pignasecca** (Via Pignasecca; 8am-1pm; M Toledo) is one of the best places to soak up the city's animated street life. Located in the Montesanto district, just north of the Quartieri Spagnoli, the market is a veritable larder for locals, all of whom swear by their favourite *fruttivendolo* (grocer), *macellaio* (butcher) and *pescivendolo* (fishmonger). Hunt down fresh pasta, local fish, fruit and vegetables, robust *prosciutto* and *salsiccie* (sausages). For superfresh *provola* (provolone), hit deli **Ai Monti Lattari** (Via Pignasecca 10).

art spanning the 17th- to early 20th centuries. Star attraction is Caravaggio's mesmerising swansong, *The Martyrdom of St Ursula* (1610). Completed weeks before the artist's lonely death, the painting depicts a vengeful king of the Huns piercing the heart of his unwilling virgin bride-to-be, Ursula. (081 42 50 11; www.palazzozevallos.com; Via Toledo 185; adult/reduced €5/3; 10am-6pm Tue-Fri, to 8pm Sat & Sun; M Municipio)

Galleria Umberto I ARCHITECTURE

3 MAP P58, C5

Recalling Milan's Galleria Vittorio Emanuele, Naples' most famous 19th-century arcade is a breathtaking pairing of richly adorned neo-Renaissance fronts and a delicate glass ceiling capped by a lofty 56m dome. Complete with a sumptuous marble floor, the *galleria* is at its most spectacular at night, when it becomes a surreal setting for impromptu soccer games. (Via San Carlo; R2 to Via San Carlo, M Municipio)

Toledo Metro Station PUBLIC ART

4 MAP P58, C4

William Kentridge's monumental equestrian statue trumpets entry to this award-winning, jaw-dropping Metro Art Station, then his dazzling mosaic of shadowy characters parades across the lobby with Naples' patron saint, San Gennaro, its grand marshal. Along the 50m descent into the bowels of the station, dark becomes light, the earth morphs into the sea and, at the bottom, waves (in the form of Robert Wilson's light-panel installation) carry passengers to the below-sea-level platform. Visit www.anm.it/infoarte@anm.it for more information about Naples metro works of art and tours. (800 639525; www.anm.it; Via Toledo; metro ticket €1.10; 6am-11pm; M Toledo)

Castel Nuovo CASTLE

5 MAP P58, D5

Locals know this 13th-century castle as the Maschio Angioino (Angevin Keep) and its Cappella Palatina is home to fragments of frescoes by Giotto; they're on the splays of the Gothic windows. You'll also find Roman ruins under the glass-floored Sala dell'Armeria (Armoury Hall). The castle's upper floors (closed on Sunday) house a collection of mostly 17th- to early 20th-century Neapolitan paintings. The top floor houses the more interesting works, including landscape paintings by Luigi Crisconio and a watercolour by architect Carlo Vanvitelli. (081 795 77 22; Piazza Municipio; adult/reduced €6/3; 8.30am-6pm Mon-Sat, 10am-1pm Sun; M Municipio)

Eating

Sfogliatella Mary — PASTRIES €

6 MAP P58, C5

At the Via Toledo entrance to Galleria Umberto I, this tiny takeaway vendor is widely considered the queen of the *sfogliatella*. Usually still warm from the oven, it's available in *riccia* (filo-style pastry) and *frolla* (shortcrust pastry) forms, both defined by a perfect balance of textures and flavours. (sfogliatelle €1.80; 8am-8.30pm Tue-Sun; R2 to Via San Carlo, M Municipio)

Antica Pizzeria e Trattoria al '22 — NEAPOLITAN €

7 MAP P58, C3

Despite its pizza-centric menu, familial Al '22 is famous for its *parmigiana di melanzane* (aubergine parmigiana), baked in terracotta ramekins and fired in the wood-fired oven. The result is a crisp, charred top that seals the cheesy, gooey bliss beneath. The pizza selection is ample, with spin-offs including golden, fried calzoni stuffed with combos like *provola* and sautéed escarole. (081 552 27 26; www.al22pizzeria.it; Via Pignasecca 22; pizzas from €4, meals €16-25; 11am-4pm & 6.30-11.30pm Mon-Thu, to 11.45pm Fri & Sat; M Toledo)

Antica Pizza Fritta da Zia Esterina Sorbillo — PIZZA €

8 MAP P58, C6

This takeaway hot spot serves up huge, superlative *pizza fritta*, deep-fried pizza dough traditionally filled with pork *cicoli* (dried lard cubes), *provola*, ricotta and tomato. A handful of variations are available, all made fresh to

Osteria della Mattonella

In Italian, *mattonella* means 'tile', an apt name for this classic Neapolitan **osteria** (Map p58, B6; 081 41 65 41; Via Giovanni Nicotera 13; meals €15-25; 12.30am-4pm & 7.30-11.30pm Mon-Sat, 12.30-4pm Sun; ; E6 to Via Giovanni Nicotera), its walls clad in 18th-century majolica tiles. Matriarch Antonietta has been running the place since 1978, her faithful regulars here for comforting, home-cooked classics. The *primi* (first courses) are particularly notable, from the *ragù* and *pasta e provola* to lentil and broccoli *zuppa* (soup).

order using organic flour and high-quality ingredients. And while it is filling, it's also surprisingly light: the key to a perfect rendition of this Neapolitan classic. (☎ 081 442 13 64; www.sorbillo.it; Piazza Trieste e Trento 53; pizza fritta from €3.50; ⏲11am-10pm Mon-Thu, to 11pm Fri & Sun, to midnight Sat; 🚌 R2 to Via San Carlo, Ⓜ Municipio)

Drinking

Caffè Gambrinus CAFE

9 MAP P58, C6

Gambrinus is Naples' oldest and most venerable cafe, serving superlative Neapolitan coffee under flouncy chandeliers. Oscar Wilde knocked back a few here and Mussolini had some rooms shut to keep out left-wing intellectuals. Sit-down prices are steep, but the *aperitivo* nibbles are decent and sipping a *spritz* or a luscious *cioccolata calda* (hot chocolate) in its belle-époque rooms is something worth savouring. (☎ 081 41 75 82; www.grancaffegambrinus.com; Via Chiaia 1-2; ⏲7am-1am Sun-Thu, to 2am Fri & Sat; 🚌 R2 to Via San Carlo, Ⓜ Municipio)

Il Birraiuolo BAR

10 MAP P58, C2

Should you swill a barrel-aged saison from the Veneto's Crak, a Tasmanian IPA from Lombardy's Hop Skin, or jump the border and down a Pannepot Grand Reserva from Belgium's De Struise Brouwers? It's the kind of conundrum you'll face at this intimate, affable temple to craft brews. Staff are

Caffè Gambrinus

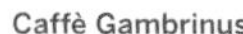

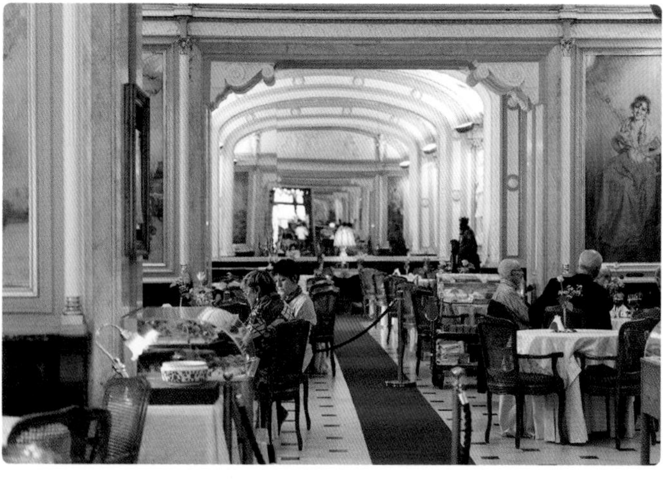

SAVVAPANF PHOTO/SHUTTERSTOCK ©

clued up about what they pour and you'll also find a solid selection of whiskies. (081 549 27 03; www.facebook.com/ilbirraiuolo; Via Bellini 48; 6.30pm-midnight Wed, Thu & Sun, to 2am Fri & Sat; M Dante)

Caffè Mexico CAFE

11 MAP P58, C2

One of Naples' best (and best-loved) coffee bars – even the local cops stop by for a quick pick-me-up – is a retro-tastic combo of old-school baristas, an orange espresso machine and velvety, full-flavoured *caffè*. The espresso is served *zuccherato* (sweetened), so request it *amaro* if you fancy a bitter hit. For an in-the-know treat, request a *harem con panna* (an Arabica bean espresso topped with luscious cream and devoured with a teaspoon). There's another branch at Piazza Garibaldi 72. (Piazza Dante 86; 5.30am-8.30pm Mon-Sat, 6.30am-2.30pm Sun; M Dante)

Entertainment

Centro di Musica Antica Pietà de' Turchini CLASSICAL MUSIC

12 MAP P58, A5

Classical-music buffs are in for a treat at this beautiful deconsecrated church, an evocative setting for concerts of mostly 17th- to 19th-century Neapolitan works. Upcoming concerts are listed on the venue's website. Note that some concerts are held at other venues, including the Palazzo Zevallos Stigliano (p59). (081 40 23 95; www.turchini.it; Via Santa Caterina da Siena 38; adult/reduced €10/7; Centrale to Corso Vittorio Emanuele)

Bourbon Street JAZZ

13 MAP P58, C2

Bourbon Street is one of the top spots for live jazz and blues, drawing a mixed crowd of seasoned jazz nerds and rookies. Acts are mostly local, with Wednesday nights dedicated to 'JamJazz', when musicians hit the stage for impromptu collaborations. Check the venue's Facebook page (Bourbon Street Napoli Jazz Club) to see who's up next. (338 8253756; www.bourbonstreetjazzclub.com; Via Bellini 52; 8.30pm-2am Tue-Thu & Sun, to 3am Fri & Sat, closed Jul-early Sep; M Dante)

Shopping

Talarico FASHION & ACCESSORIES

14 MAP P58, C4

Mario Talarico and his nephew have turned the humble umbrella into a work of art. Sought after by heads of state, each piece is a one-off, with mother-of-pearl buttons, a horn tip and a handle made from a single tree branch. While top-of-the-range pieces can fetch €500, there are more affordable options that will keep the budget-conscious singing in the rain. (081 40 77 23; www.mariotalarico.it; Vico Due Porte a Toledo 4b; 8am-8pm Mon-Sat; M Toledo)

La Sanità & Capodimonte

La Sanità was for centuries where the city buried its dead. These days, its jumble of bassi *(one-room, ground-floor houses), frescoed catacombs and baroque staircases pull an ever-growing number of resident artists and bohemians, drawn to the neighbourhood's textures and raw energy. To the north is Capodimonte, famed for its art-crammed palace.*

The Catacombe di San Gennaro (p69) and Catacombe di San Gaudioso (p69) are covered by the same ticket and both run guided tours. A 1km walk west of the latter is the Cimitero delle Fontanelle (p69). The baroque staircases of Palazzo Sanfelice (p70) and Palazzo dello Spagnolo (p69) are also within walking distance of the Catacombe di San Gaudioso and close to pizzeria Concettina Ai Tre Santi (p70). North of La Sanità is Palazzo Reale di Capodimonte (p66) and the Parco di Capodimonte (p67), which merit half a day.

Getting There & Around

M Piazza Cavour station (Line 2) skirts the southern edge of La Sanità, running west to Chiaia (Piazza Amedeo) and Mergellina and east to Napoli Centrale. It's connected to Museo station (Line 1), useful for Vomero (Piazza Vanvitelli) and Municipio.

Route C51 runs through La Sanità to Cimitero delle Fontanelle. Routes R2 and 178 run north along Via Toledo to Catacombe di San Gennaro and Capodimonte.

La Sanità & Capodimonte Map on p68

Palazzo dello Spagnolo (p69) LAURADIBI/SHUTTERSTOCK ©

Top Experience

Wander the Palazzo Reale di Capodimonte

Originally designed as a hunting lodge for Charles VII of Bourbon, this monumental palace was begun in 1738 and took more than a century to complete. It's now home to Museo e Real Bosco di Capodimonte – southern Italy's largest and richest art gallery. Waiting beyond it is the Parco di Capodimonte, Naples' glorious, green, panoramic lungs.

MAP P68, C2

www.museocapodimonte.beniculturali.it

Via Miano 2

adult/reduced €12/8

8.30am-7.30pm Thu-Tue

R4, 178 to Via Capodimonte, shuttle bus Shuttle Capodimonte

Museum Masterpieces

The museum constitutes a number of historic collections, most notably the Farnese Collection, inherited by Charles VII of Bourbon from his mother, Elisabetta Farnese. First-floor highlights include Masaccio's shimmering *Crucifixion,* Botticelli's *Madonna with Child and Angels,* Bellini's *Transfiguration* and Parmigianino's *Antea,* all of which are subject to room changes within the museum. Rooms 31 to 60 constitute the Appartamento Reale (Royal Apartment), with two royal portraits by Goya in Room 34 and the outrageous porcelain chinoiserie of the Salottino di Porcellana (Room 52). Second-floor highlights include a series of early 16th-century tapestries depicting the 1525 Battle of Pavia, a pivotal moment in the Italian War of 1521–26. Caravaggio's *Flagellation of Christ* entrances in Room 78, while rooms 88 to 95 offer a feast of Neapolitan baroque paintings. Accessed from the 2nd floor, a small mezzanine level hosts rotating modern works from artists including Andy Warhol and John Armleder.

Parco di Capodimonte

Designed by Ferdinando Sanfelice in 1742 as a royal hunting reserve, the **Parco di Capodimonte** (www.boscodicapodimonte.it; admission free; 7.30am-7.30pm Apr-Sep, to 6pm Feb, Mar & Oct, to 5pm Nov-Jan) sprawls across 134 hectares in a series of themed gardens and woods. East of the palace building lies the park's Porta di Mezzo (Middle Gate), from where five paths radiate out into the woods in one of the finest examples of late-baroque garden architecture. The central path leads to the *Statua del Gigante* (Statue of the Giant), named for its colossal dimensions. This is the park's most valuable sculpture; its ancient bust, head and vase transferred to Naples' from the Palazzo Farnese in Rome in 1763. The palace website includes a map of the park, complete with a series of themed walks.

★ Top Tips

- Buy some fresh bread, cheese, *salumi* (cured meats) and fruit from Naples' La Pignasecca market (p60) before heading here, to enjoy a picnic in the park.
- The museum has a little-known collection of 19th-century art, as well as works by prolific Neapolitan photographer Mimmo Jodice. To request a viewing, email mu-cap.accoglienza.capodimonte@beniculturali.it in advance.

✕ Take a Break

- The museum houses a courtyard cafe, selling pastries, *panini,* snacks and both alcoholic and nonalcoholic beverages.
- For pizza and pasta dishes, cross the street and settle in at casual **Da Luisa** (081 44 97 66; Via Capodimonte 19; pizzas from €3, meals €18; noon-3.30pm & 7-11pm Tue-Sun).

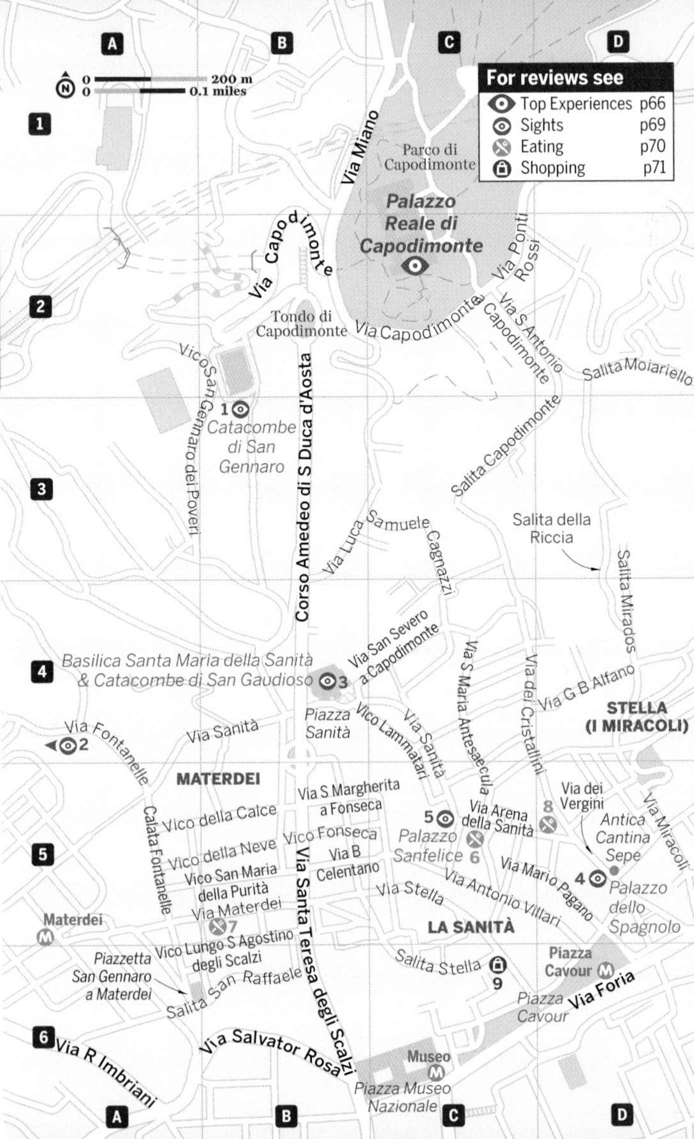

A
B
C
D
0 200 m
0 0.1 miles
1
2
3
4
5
6
For reviews see
Top Experiences p66
Sights p69
Eating p70
Shopping p71
Via Miano
Parco di Capodimonte
Palazzo Reale di Capodimonte
Via Capodimonte
Via Ponti Rossi
Tondo di Capodimonte
Via Capodimonte
Via S Antonio a Capodimonte
Salita Moiariello
Vico San Gennaro dei Poveri
1 Catacombe di San Gennaro
Corso Amedeo di S Duca d'Aosta
Salita Capodimonte
Via Luca Samuele Cagnazzi
Salita della Riccia
Salita Mirados
Via San Severo a Capodimonte
Basilica Santa Maria della Sanità & Catacombe di San Gaudioso 3
Via S Maria Antesaecula
Via dei Cristallini
Via G B Alfano
STELLA (I MIRACOLI)
Via Fontanelle
2
Via Sanità
Piazza Sanità
Vico Lammatari
Via Sanità
MATERDEI
Via S Margherita a Fonseca
5
Via Arena della Sanità
8
Via dei Vergini
Antica Cantina Sepe
Via Miracoli
Calata Fontanelle
Vico della Calce
Vico della Neve
Vico Fonseca
Via B Celentano
Palazzo Sanfelice 6
Vico San Maria della Purità
Via Santa Teresa degli Scalzi
Via Mario Pagano
4 Palazzo dello Spagnolo
Via Materdei
7
Via Stella
Via Antonio Villari
Materdei
LA SANITÀ
Vico Lungo S Agostino degli Scalzi
Piazzetta San Gennaro a Materdei
Salita San Raffaele
Salita Stella
9
Piazza Cavour
Piazza Cavour
Via Foria
Via R Imbriani
Via Salvator Rosa
Museo
Piazza Museo Nazionale

Sights

Catacombe di San Gennaro CATACOMB

1 MAP P68, B3

Naples' oldest and most sacred catacombs became a Christian pilgrimage site when San Gennaro's body was interred here in the 5th century. The carefully restored site allows visitors to experience an evocative other world of tombs, corridors and broad vestibules, its treasures including 2nd-century Christian frescoes, 5th-century mosaics and the oldest known portrait of San Gennaro, dating from the second half of the 5th century. (081 744 37 14; www.catacombedinapoli.it; Via Capodimonte 13; adult/reduced €9/6; 1hr tours hourly 10am-5pm Mon-Sat, to 2pm Sun; R4, 178 to Via Capodimonte)

Cimitero delle Fontanelle CEMETERY

2 MAP P68, A4

Holding about eight million human bones, the ghoulish Fontanelle Cemetery was first used during the 1656 plague, before becoming Naples' main burial site during the 1837 cholera epidemic. At the end of the 19th century it became a hot spot for the *anime pezzentelle* (poor souls) cult, in which locals adopted skulls and prayed for their souls. Lack of information at the site makes joining a tour much more rewarding; **Cooperativa Sociale Onlus 'La Paranza'** (081 744 37 14; www.catacombedinapoli.it; Via Capodimonte 13; information point 10am-5pm Mon-Sat, to 2pm Sun; R4, 178 to Via Capodimonte) are among the reputable outfits. (081 1970 3197; www.cimiterofontanelle.com; Via Fontanelle 80; admission free; 10am-5pm; C51 to Via Fontanelle, M Materdei)

Basilica Santa Maria della Sanità & Catacombe di San Gaudioso CHURCH, CATACOMB

3 MAP P68, B4

While we love the baroque paintings by Andrea Vaccaro and Luca Giordano – not to mention the two contemporary sculptures by Riccardo Dalisi – it's the eerie catacombs beneath this 17th-century basilica that makes the place so utterly unforgettable. Entered through the 5th-century **cripta** (crypt) below the high altar, its damp walls reveal a rather macabre method of medieval burial. (081 744 37 14; www.catacombedinapoli.it; Piazza Sanità 14; basilica free, catacomb adult/reduced €9/6; basilica 9am-1pm, 1hr catacomb tours 10am, 11am, noon & 1pm; C51 to Piazza Sanità, M Piazza Cavour, Museo)

Palazzo dello Spagnolo ARCHITECTURE

4 MAP P68, D5

In baroque-rich Naples, even staircases can be an event and the masterpiece gracing the courtyard of this *palazzo* is one of its most show-stopping. Designed by Ferdinando Sanfelice and dating from 1738, its double-ramped, five-arched flights were put to good use in film classics such as Luigi Zampa's *Processo alla città* (The City Stands Trial) and Vittorio de Sica's *Giudizio universale* (The Last Judgment). (Via dei Vergini 19; C51, C52 to Via dei Vergini, M Piazza Cavour)

Palazzo Sanfelice ARCHITECTURE

5 MAP P68, C5

Ferdinando Sanfelice's debut staircase is this double-ramped diva inside the Palazzo Sanfelice. Upon its completion in 1726 it became the talk of the town, and from then on there was no stopping Sanfelice, who perfected his dramatic design in various *palazzi* across the city, culminating in his masterpiece at the Palazzo dello Spagnolo (p69). (Via Arena della Sanità 6; C51, C52 to Via Arena della Sanità, M Piazza Cavour)

Eating

Concettina Ai Tre Santi PIZZA €

6 MAP P68, C5

Head in by noon (or 7.30pm at dinner) to avoid a long wait at this hot spot pizzeria, made famous thanks to its young, driven *pizzaiolo* Ciro Oliva. The menu is an index of fastidiously sourced artisanal ingredients, used to top Ciro's flawless, wood-fired bases. Traditional Neapolitan pizza aside, you'll also find a string of creative seasonal options. (081 29 00 37;

Palazzo Sanfelice

SIMONA FLAMIGNI/SHUTTERSTOCK ©

www.pizzeriaoliva.it; Via Arena della Sanità 7; pizzas from €5; noon-midnight Mon-Sat, to 5pm Sun; ; M Piazza Cavour, Museo)

Pizzeria Starita PIZZA €

7 MAP P68, B5

The giant fork and ladle hanging on the wall at this historic pizzeria were used by Sophia Loren in *L'oro di Napoli*, and the kitchen made the *pizze fritte* sold by the actress in the film. While the 60-plus pizza varieties include a tasty *fiorilli e zucchine* (zucchini, zucchini flowers and *provola*), our allegiance remains to its classic marinara. (081 557 36 82; www.pizzeriestarita.it; Via Materdei 28; pizzas from €3.50; noon-3.30pm & 7pm-midnight Tue-Sun; M Materdei)

Pasticceria Poppella PASTRIES €

8 MAP P68, D5

Neapolitans from across the city revere this light, upbeat pastry shop for its *fiocco di neve* (snowflake), a soft, small brioche, dusted in icing sugar and packed with a deceptively light, vanilla-scented filling of ricotta and Italian pastry cream. While it is Poppella's undisputed highlight, you'll also find all the usual suspects, from rum-soaked *babà* to creamy cannoli pimped with glacé cherries. (081 45 53 09; www.facebook.com/pasticceriapoppella; Via Arena della Sanità 29; 6am-10pm; M Piazza Cavour, Museo)

Cheap Vino, Homely Aperitivo

Pocket-sized cantina and grocery store **Antica Cantina Sepe** (Map p68, D5; 081 45 46 09; Via dei Vergini 55; 9am-8.30pm, to midnight Thu; M Piazza Cavour, Museo) has become an unlikely hot spot thanks to next-gen owner, Francesco Sepe, and his on-tap local vino, sold at €1.50 a glass. Fancier wines cost no more than €3.50 a pop, while Thursday nights see mamma Giovanna make a small feast for the weekly *aperitivo* session, which features DJ sets, live music or other cultural events.

Shopping

Omega FASHION & ACCESSORIES

9 MAP P68, C6

Despite hiding away on the 3rd floor of a nondescript building, Paris, New York and Tokyo know all about this family-run glove factory, whose clients include Dior and Hermes. Omega's men's and women's leather gloves are meticulously handcrafted using a traditional 25-step process and, best of all, they retail for a fraction of the price charged by the luxury fashion houses. (081 29 90 41; www.omegasrl.com; Via Stella 12; 8.30am-6pm Mon-Fri; M Piazza Cavour, Museo)

Walking Tour

The Vomero Good Life

A quick funicular ride away from central Naples, mild-mannered Vomero is the city's middle-class epicentre, a hilltop enclave of broad, gridded streets, neoclassical palazzi *and cafe-lounging Neapolitans. Head up here for a slightly slower pace of life, one which will have you scanning racks for cognoscenti labels, sipping single-origin espresso in a maverick cafe, and whetting your appetite in a classic neighbourhood market.*

Getting There

Centrale to Piazza Fuga

M Vanvitelli

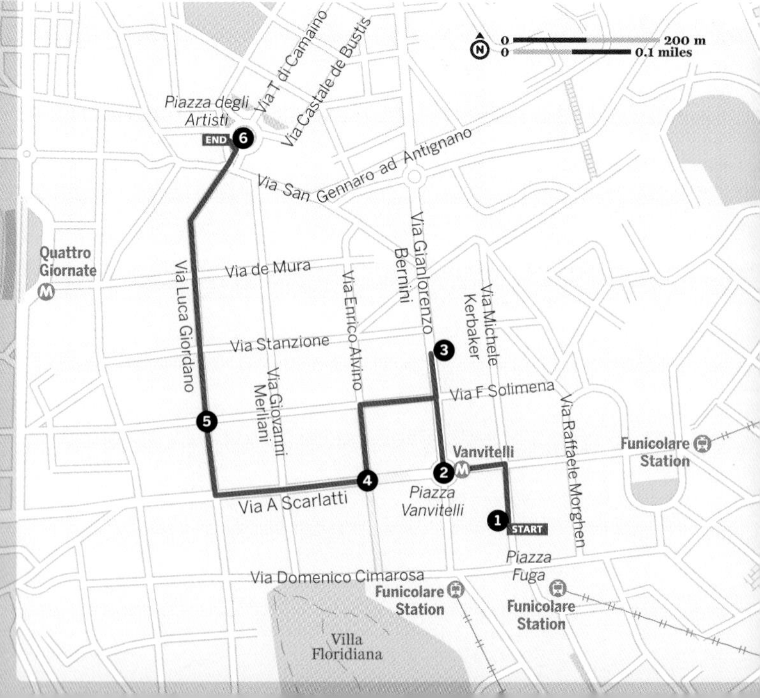

❶ Riot Laundry Bar

Score hip streetwear, vinyl and a coffee at **Riot Laundry Bar** (☎081 1957 8491; www.facebook.com/riotlaundrybarandclothes; Via Kerbaker 19; ⏰shop 10am-2pm & 4-8pm Mon-Thu, to midnight Fri, 10am-midnight Sat, cafe/bar 8am-2am Mon-Thu & Sun, to 4am Fri & Sat), one of Naples' few concept stores. Labels include Denmark's Wood Wood and France's Libertine and co-owner Stefano also stocks his own denim label Derriere Heritage, which offers customised cuts, washes and detailing.

❷ Piazza Vanvitelli

Octagonal, cafe-speckled **Piazza Vanvitelli** draws respectable, middle-class families. In the evenings, metro-riding teens pour in from the northern suburbs, their parents preferring that they socialise here rather than in the edgier *centro storico*. The neo-Renaissance *palazzi* flanking the piazza are top-tier real estate.

❸ Ventimetriquadri

A guest from Melbourne, Australia, introduced Vincenzo Fioretto to specialty coffee, igniting a passion that led to him opening **Ventimetriquadri** (☎345 5328421; www.facebook.com/ventimetriquadri.specialtycoffee; Via Bernini 64A; ⏰3-11pm Mon, 9am-11pm Tue-Fri, 10am-midnight Sat, 10am-2pm & 6-11pm Sun; 📶), Naples' first specialty-coffee cafe. Chances are you'll find 'Enzo' behind the counter, grinding single-origin beans to order. Try a coffee from Pompeii-based roaster Campana.

❹ Via Scarlatti

Car-free **Via Scarlatti** is flanked by cafes, chain stores and heirloom family businesses. Its infamous fountain – derisively likened to a market tub for eels by some locals – was removed in 2018, much to the indignation of its creator, Ernesto Tatafiore. Off Via Scarlatti, Via Alvino claims two retro icons: the Televomero sign (for a local TV channel) and Caffè Salvo.

❺ Via Giordano

Named in honour of Neapolitan baroque painter Luca Giordano, **Via Giordano** is peppered with shops, cafes and the odd historic villa. The kiosks on the block between Via Stanzione and Via De Mura sell books (mostly in Italian) and film poster prints, including Italian-language versions of Hollywood classics.

❻ Mercatino di Antignano

On the evening of 23 December, the **Mercatino di Antignano** (Piazza degli Artisti; ⏰7am-1.30pm Mon-Sat) becomes a battlefield as locals push and shove to snap up the freshest seafood for their Christmas Eve feasts. Throughout the year, it's where they head for everything from linen and bags to *stocco* (air-dried cod), olives and vegetables.

Worth a Trip

View Treasures at Certosa e Museo di San Martino

What was once a panoramic home for Carthusian monks is now a bastion of Neapolitan art and ingenuity. Home to stunning baroque interiors and one of the country's finest cloisters, its eclectic array of treasures includes precious paintings, royal barges and an important collection of presepi napoletani *(Neapolitan nativity cribs), together offering insight into the city's richly textured past.*

081 229 45 03

www.polomuseale campania.beniculturali.it

Largo San Martino 5

adult/reduced €6/3

8.30am-7.30pm Thu-Tue

M Vanvitelli, Montesanto to Morghen

Chiesa della Certosa

The Certosa's church is one of Naples' most impressive baroque assets. Both the facade and the interior's spectacular inlaid marble were designed by Cosimo Fanzago, commissioned to restructure the Certosa between 1623 and 1656. The wooden choir from 1629 is by Orazio De Orio, while the marble statues representing Courage and Charity were executed by Giuseppe Sanmartino, sculptor of the *Cristo velato* in Naples' Cappella Sansevero. The sacristy wows with ceiling frescoes by Cavalier d'Arpino, while the Cappella del Tesoro houses Jusepe de Ribera's *Pietà* and Luca Giordano's vault masterpiece *Triumph of Judith*.

Chiostro Grande

Designed by Giovanni Antonio Dosio in the late 16th century and revamped by Cosimo Fanzago in the 17th century, the Chiostro Grande is widely considered one of the finest cloisters in Italy. Refined Tuscan-Doric porticoes frame the courtyard, itself dotted with vibrant camellias. The balustrade – capped by skulls designed by Fanzago – marks the area once used as the monastery's cemetery.

Cultural Treasures

The Certosa's precious objects are divided into various galleries. The section *Immagini e Memorie di Napoli della Città e del Regno di Napoli* (Images and Memories of the City and Kingdom of Naples) is home to the *Tavola Strozzi*, a detailed oil-on-wood depiction of 15th-century Naples. The Sezione Navale houses a small but important collection of royal barges, while the Sezione Presepiale is famous for its colossal Presepe Cuciniello, arguably the most important of all the city's *presepi* (nativity cribs). The Quarto del Priore is home to Pietro Bernini's sculpture *Madonna and Child with the Infant John the Baptist*.

★ Top Tips

- Try to avoid visiting after 5pm or on Sunday – fewer staff means a greater chance of some sections being closed.
- Don't miss the sweeping view from the Loggia del Priore in the Quarto del Priore gallery, taking in the Prior's private garden, the eastern side of Naples and Mt Vesuvius.

Take a Break

- For specialty coffee or wine, craft beer and grazing platters, hit Ventimetriquadri (p73) in central Vomero.
- Golden Neapolitan street food is the drawcard at takeaway **Friggitoria Vomero** (081 578 31 30; Via Domenico Cimarosa 44; snacks from €0.25; 8.30am-2.30pm & 5-9pm Mon-Fri, to 11pm Sat; M Vanvitelli, Centrale to Piazza Fuga), also in central Vomero.

Santa Lucia & Chiaia

Fin-de-siècle hotels, the hulking Castel dell'Ovo and seaside vistas define Santa Lucia, a compact, respectable district anchored by Via Santa Lucia. This is the place for waterfront passeggiate *(strolls) and seafood feasts by bobbing boats. Sprawling to the west of Santa Lucia is Chiaia, home to high-end boutiques, bar-packed side streets, fashionable Neapolitans and a former Rothschild villa.*

Snoop around the Museo Pignatelli (p82) before strolling along the Lungomare to the Castel dell'Ovo (p82). If you're peckish, feast at waterfront Trattoria Castel dell'Ovo (p86) or tucked-away Officina del Mare (p86). Backtrack along the Lungomare to Via Domenico Morelli to join the 3.30pm tour of the Galleria Borbonica (p82). After the tour, window-shop along Via Chiaia, Via Cavallerizza a Chiaia and Via Filangieri (which becomes Via dei Mille) and peek at the dramatic elliptical staircase inside Palazzo Mannajuolo (p82). Come evening, rehydrate at the aperitivo bars south of Via Cavallerizza a Chiaia.

Getting There & Around

Route 140 runs to Mergellina and Posillipo. Route E6 runs to Piazza Trieste e Trento.

M From Piazza Amedeo station, Line 2 heads west to Mergellina and east to Montesanto, Piazza Cavour (useful for both La Sanità and *centro storico*) and Napoli Centrale.

The Funicolare di Chiaia connects Chiaia to Vomero.

Santa Lucia & Chiaia Map on p80

Villa Comunale (p83) GREG ELMS/LONELY PLANET ©

Walking Tour

Chiaia to Santa Lucia

Chiaia and Santa Lucia offer an unexpected take on Naples. Here, earthy, washing-strung backstreets play second fiddle to elegant art nouveau buildings, chic boutiques and panoramic bay views. So style up and take a saunter through a Napoli that revels in grandeur, finery and fare bella figura (making a good impression).

Walk Facts

Start Piazza Amedeo; M Piazza Amedeo

End Castel dell'Ovo; E6, 128 to Via Santa Lucia

Length 2.2km; 1½ hours

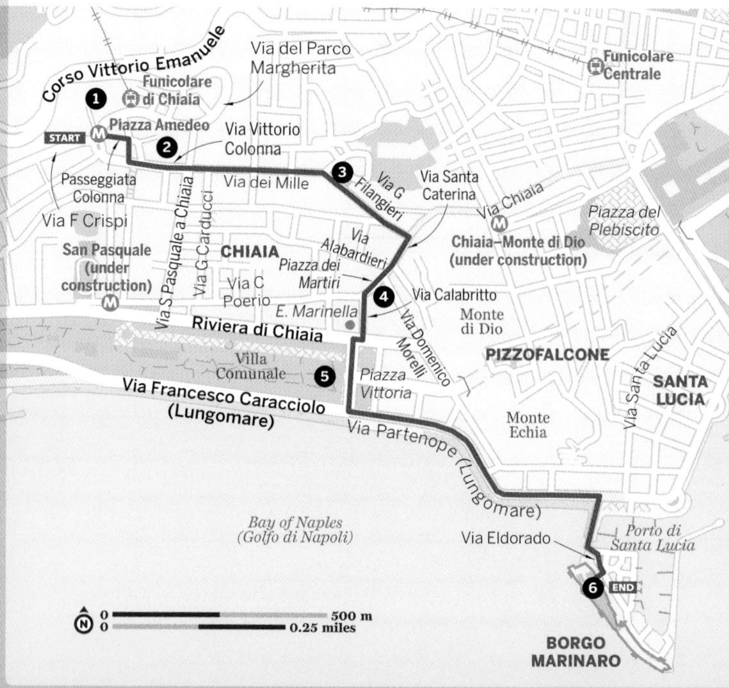

❶ Villa Maria

Just off the northern end of Piazza Amedeo, colourful **Villa Maria** is an outstanding example of Italian art nouveau architecture. Dating from 1901, the building was commissioned by French entrepreneur Giulio Huraut and designed by Veneto architect Angelo Trevisan as the Grand Eden Hotel, a luxury slumber pad for wealthy foreign travellers.

❷ Chiesa di Santa Teresa a Chiaia

From the piazza, slip into **Passeggiata Colonna**, an outdoor arcade flanked by small boutiques. Turn left into Via Vittorio Colonna (which becomes Via dei Mille) and you'll pass the unapologetically baroque **Chiesa di Santa Teresa a Chiaia** (☎081 41 42 63; Via Vittorio Colonna 22; ⏲7.30-11am Mon-Sat, 8.30am-noon & 5-7.30pm Sun), designed by Cosimo Fanzago and home to paintings by Luca Giordano.

❸ Palazzo Mannajuolo

Via dei Mille eventually kinks southeast, becoming Via Filangieri. It's here that you'll find art nouveau **Palazzo Mannajuolo** (p82). Wander inside to admire its spiral staircase, famously featured in *Napoli velata* (Naples in Veils), a film by prolific Turkish-Italian director Ferzan Özpetek.

❹ Piazza dei Martiri

At the end of Via Filangieri, turn right into Via Santa Caterina. The street spills into **Piazza dei Martiri**, its 19th-century centrepiece dedicated to Neapolitan martyrs. The monument's four lions represent the anti-Bourbon uprisings of 1799, 1820, 1848 and 1860. Palazzo Calabritto (No 30) was designed by architect Luigi Vanvitelli, famous for his monumental Reggia di Caserta.

❺ Villa Comunale

Head south on exclusive Via Calabritto and turn right into Riviera di Chiaia to drop into historic atelier **E. Marinella** (☎081 764 32 65; www.emarinella.com; Via Riviera di Chiaia 287; ⏲6.30am-8pm Mon-Sat, 9am-1pm Sun), world-famous for its silk ties. Across the street is former Bourbon garden **Villa Comunale** (p83). Dividing the Riviera di Chiaia from Via Caracciolo and the sea, this is the neighbourhood's communal backyard, complete with roller-skating rink and bandstand.

❻ Castel dell'Ovo

Turn left into **Via Partenope** (Lungomare), a pedestrianised seafront promenade popular with everyone from love-struck couples to Neapolitan families. The strip leads to Via Eldorado and the ancient islet of Borgo Marinaro, home to the **Castel dell'Ovo** (p82) and its silver-screen-worthy rooftop views.

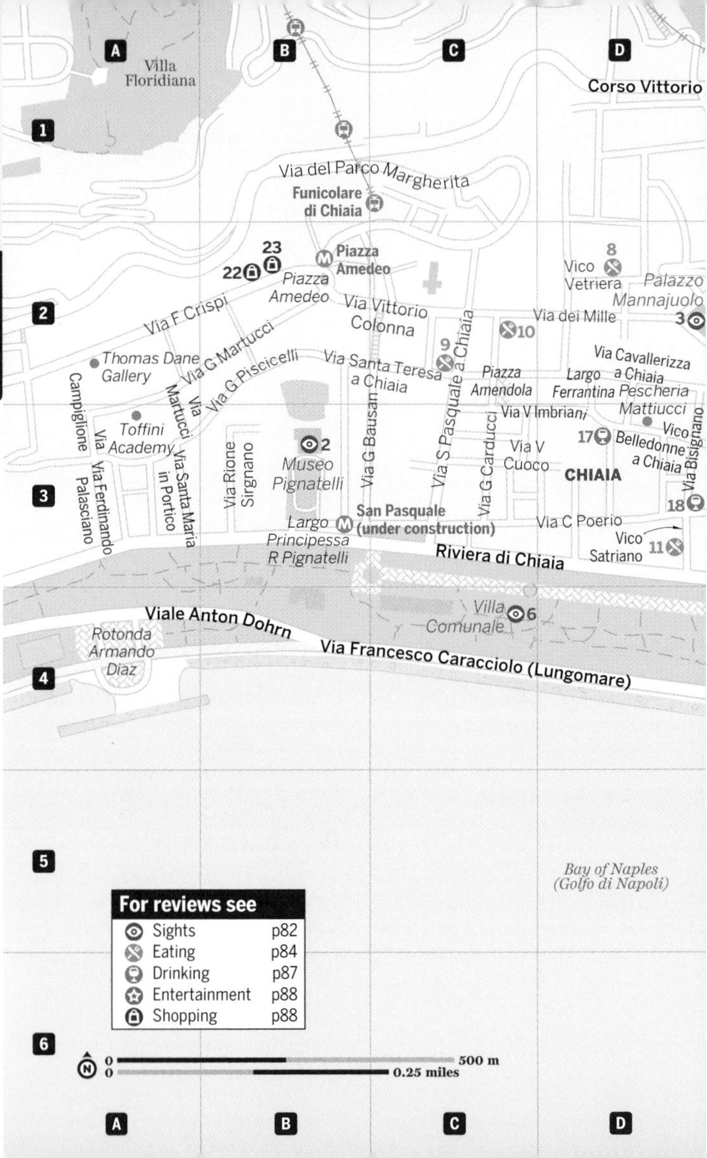

A B C D
1 2 3 4 5 6

Villa Floridiana
Corso Vittorio
Via del Parco Margherita
Funicolare di Chiaia
23
22
Piazza Amedeo
Piazza Amedeo
8
Vico Vetriera
Palazzo Mannajuolo
3
Via F Crispi
Via Vittorio Colonna
Via dei Mille
10
Via G Martucci
9
Via Cavallerizza a Chiaia
Thomas Dane Gallery
Via G Piscicelli
Via Santa Teresa a Chiaia
Piazza Amendola
Largo Ferrantina
Pescheria Mattiucci
Campiglione
Via Martucci
Via
Via V Imbriani
Toffini Academy
Via
2
Via G Bausan
Via S Pasquale a Chiaia
Via G Carducci
17
Vico Belledonne a Chiaia
Via Bisignano
Via V Cuoco
CHIAIA
Via Rione Sirgnano
Museo Pignatelli
Via Ferdinando Palasciano
Via Santa Maria in Portico
18
San Pasquale (under construction)
Largo Principessa R Pignatelli
Via C Poerio
Vico Satriano
11
Riviera di Chiaia
Villa Comunale
6
Viale Anton Dohrn
Rotonda Armando Diaz
Via Francesco Caracciolo (Lungomare)
Bay of Naples (Golfo di Napoli)

For reviews see

Sights	p82
Eating	p84
Drinking	p87
Entertainment	p88
Shopping	p88

0 500 m
0 0.25 miles

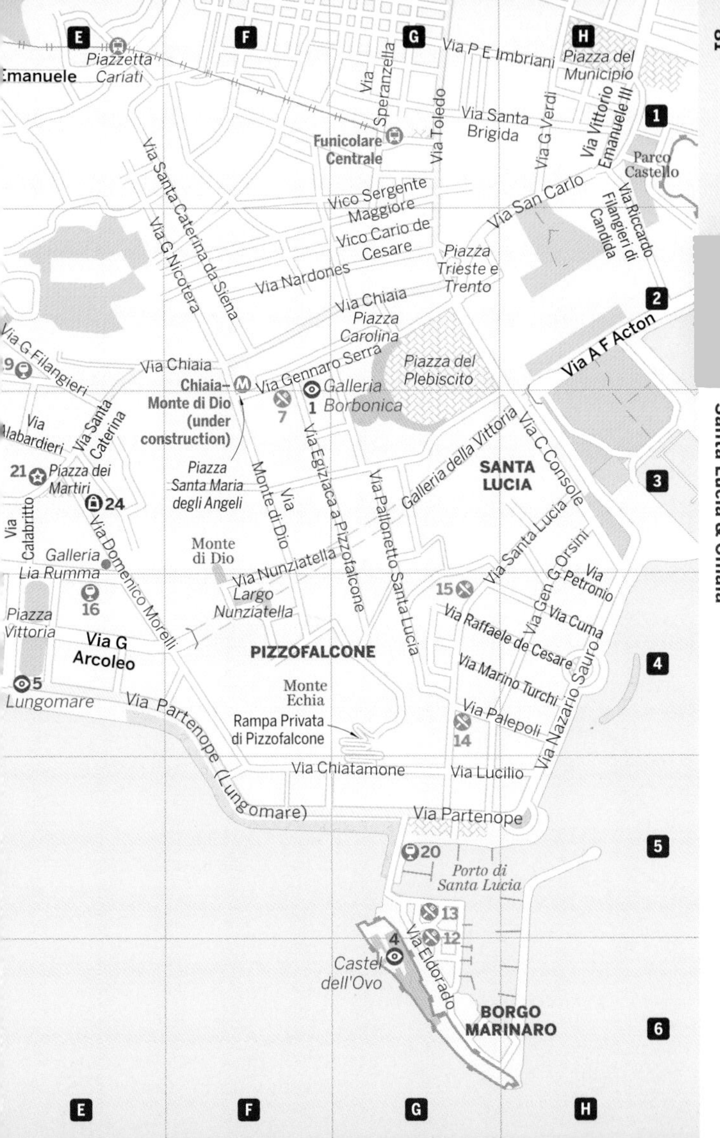
E
F
G
H
1
2
3
4
5
6
Piazzetta Cariati
Emanuele
Via P E Imbriani
Piazza del Municipio
Via Speranzella
Via Toledo
Via Santa Brigida
Via G Verdi
Via Vittorio Emanuele III
Parco Castello
Funicolare Centrale
Via Santa Caterina da Siena
Via G Nicotera
Vico Sergente Maggiore
Vico Cario de Cesare
Via San Carlo
Via Riccardo Filangieri di Candida
Piazza Trieste e Trento
Via Nardones
Via Chiaia
Piazza Carolina
Via A F Acton
Via G Filangieri
9
Via Chiaia
Via Gennaro Serra
Piazza del Plebiscito
Chiaia–Monte di Dio (under construction)
7
1 Galleria Borbonica
Via Alabardieri
Via Santa Caterina
Via Galleria della Vittoria
Via C Console
SANTA LUCIA
21 Piazza dei Martiri
24
Piazza Santa Maria degli Angeli
Via Monte di Dio
Via Egiziaca a Pizzofalcone
Via Pallonetto Santa Lucia
Via Calabritto
Via Domenico Morelli
Galleria Lia Rumma
Monte di Dio
Via Nunziatella
Largo Nunziatella
Via Santa Lucia
Via Gen G Orsini
Via Petronio
15
16
Piazza Vittoria
Via G Arcoleo
Via Raffaele de Cesare
Via Cuma
PIZZOFALCONE
5 Lungomare
Via Marino Turchi
Via Nazario Sauro
Monte Echia
Via Partenope (Lungomare)
Rampa Privata di Pizzofalcone
Via Palepoli
14
Via Chiatamone
Via Lucilio
Via Partenope
20
Porto di Santa Lucia
13
12
4 Castel dell'Ovo
Via Eldorado
BORGO MARINARO

Sights

Galleria Borbonica

HISTORIC SITE

1 MAP P80, F2

Traverse five centuries along Naples' engrossing Bourbon Tunnel. Conceived by Ferdinand II in 1853 to link the Palazzo Reale (p56) to the barracks and the sea, the never-completed escape route is part of the 17th-century Carmignano Aqueduct system, itself incorporating 16th-century cisterns. The standard tour and the Via delle Memorie Tour (75 minutes; adult/reduced €10/5) do not require pre-booking, though the Adventure Tour (85 minutes; adult/reduced €15/10) and adults-only Speleo Light Tour (90 minutes; €15) do. (366 2484151, 081 764 58 08; www.galleriaborbonica.com; Vico del Grottone 4; 1hr standard tours adult/reduced €10/5; standard tours 10am, noon, 3.30pm & 5.30pm Fri-Sun; R2 to Via San Carlo)

Museo Pignatelli

MUSEUM

2 MAP P80, B3

When Ferdinand Acton, a minister at the court of King Ferdinand IV (1759–1825), asked Pietro Valente to design Villa Pignatelli in 1826, Valente whipped up this striking Pompeiian facsimile. Now the Museo Pignatelli, its aristocratic hoard includes sumptuous furniture and decorative arts, as well as a beautiful collection of 19th- and 20th-century carriages in the adjoining **Museo delle Carrozze**. (081 761 23 56; www.polomusealecampania.beniculturali.it; Riviera di Chiaia 200; adult/reduced €5/2.50; 8.30am-5pm Wed-Mon; 140 to Riviera di Chiaia)

Palazzo Mannajuolo

ARCHITECTURE

3 MAP P80, D2

Commissioned by entrepreneur and engineer Giuseppe Mannajuolo, this distinguished *palazzo* was built between 1910 and 1911. It's one of the city's finest examples of Italian art nouveau architecture, known as *stile Liberty* (Liberty style). The building's western facade is especially impressive, its alternating convex and concave elements crowned by a faux dome. The star attraction, however, is the building's cinematic indoor staircase, an astonishing elliptical creation adorned with wrought-iron parapets and embossed marble steps. (Via Filangieri 36; 8am-9pm; E6 to Piazza dei Martiri, M Piazza Amedeo)

Castel dell'Ovo

CASTLE

4 MAP P80, G6

Built by the Normans in the 12th century, Naples' oldest castle owes its name (Castle of the Egg) to Virgil. The Roman scribe reputedly buried an egg on the site where the castle now stands, warning that when the egg breaks, the castle (and Naples) will fall. Thankfully, both are still standing, and walking up to the castle's ramparts will reward you with a breathtaking panorama. (081 795 45 92; Borgo Marinaro; admission free; 9am-7pm Mon-Sat, to 1.30pm Sun Apr-Oct, reduced hours rest of year; E6, 128 to Via Santa Lucia)

Lungomare

STREET, PARK

5 MAP P80, E4

When you need a break from Naples' hyperactive tendencies, take a deep breath on its pedestrianised seafront strip. Stretching 2.5km along Via Partenope and Via Caracciolo, its views are nothing short of exquisite, taking in the bay, Mt Vesuvius, two castles and Vomero's Liberty-style villas. It's particularly romantic at dusk, when Capri and the volcano take on a mellow orange hue. (Seafront; Via Caracciolo & Via Partenope; C25 to Piazza Vittoria)

Villa Comunale

PARK

6 MAP P80, C4

Another Luigi Vanvitelli production, this long, leafy seaside strip was originally built for Bourbon royalty. Called the Passeggio Reale (Royal Walkway), it was off limits to the plebs except on 8 September, the day of the Festa di Piedigrotta. Rumour has it that taking one's wife to the park on that day was a clause in many a marital contract. Husbands across the city must have heaved a sigh of relief when the park finally went public in 1869.

Dividing the Riviera di Chiaia from Via Caracciolo and the sea, this urban oasis boasts a vintage aquarium, roller-skating rink, bandstand, tennis club and at least eight fountains. Named after the ducks that used to swim in it, the Fontana delle Paperelle (Duck Fountain) replaced the famous *Toro Farnese* (Faranese Bull) which,

Contemporary Art Galleries

Chiaia is home to two especially notable contemporary art galleries. Just west of Piazza Amedeo, prolific London import **Thomas Dane Gallery** (Map p80, A2; 081 1892 0545; www.thomasdanegallery.com; Via Crispi 69; 11am-7pm Tue-Fri, noon-7pm Sat; M Piazza Amedeo) sits inside 19th-century Villa Ruffo, which offers inspiring bay views to complement rotating exhibitions of international contemporary art. Closer to Piazza Martiri, **Galleria Lia Rumma** (Map p80, E3; 081 1981 2354; www.liarumma.it; Via Gaetani 12; 11am-1.30pm & 2.30-7pm Tue-Sat; 151, 154 to Piazza Vittoria) occupies the former apartment of its namesake gallerist and collector. Rumma is well known for discovering the next big names in art, having helped launch the careers of art-world heavyweights including Joseph Kosuth and Haim Steinbach.

SIRIO CARNEVALINO/SHUTTERSTOCK ©

Castel dell'Ovo (p82)

in 1825, was transferred to the Museo Archeologico Nazionale (p52). (Piazza Vittoria; 7am-midnight; C25 to Piazza Vittoria, 128, 140 to Riviera di Chiaia)

Eating

Da Ettore NEAPOLITAN €€

7 MAP P80, F3

This homey, eight-table trattoria has an epic reputation. Scan the walls for famous fans like comedy great Totò, and a framed passage from crime writer Massimo Siviero, who mentions Ettore in one of his tales. The draw is solid regional cooking, which includes one of the best *spaghetti alle vongole* (spaghetti with clams) in town. Book two days ahead for Sunday lunch. (081 764 35 78; Via Gennaro Serra 39; meals €25; 1-2.30pm daily, 8-10pm Tue-Sat; ; R2 to Via San Carlo)

L'Ebbrezza di Noè ITALIAN €€

8 MAP P80, D2

A wine shop by day, 'Noah's Drunkenness' transforms into an intimate culinary hot spot by night. Slip inside for vino and conversation with sommelier Luca at the bar, or settle into one of the bottle-lined dining rooms for seductive, market-driven dishes such as house special *paccheri fritti* (fried pasta stuffed with aubergine and served with fresh basil and a rich tomato sauce). (081 40 01 04; www.lebbrezzadinoe.com; Vico Vetriera 9; meals €35-40, cheese & charcuterie platters €10; 6pm-midnight Tue-Thu, to 1am Fri & Sat, noon-3pm Sun; [wi-fi]; [M] Piazza Amedeo)

Antica Osteria Da Tonino

ITALIAN €

9 MAP P80, C2

Wood-panelled, family-run Da Tonino has been feeding locals since 1880. Now run by the fifth and sixth generations, its gingham-print tables lure everyone from Rubinacci suits to old-timers and the odd Nobel Prize winner (Dario Fo ate here). The day's menu – hand-written and photocopied – offers simple, beautiful home-cooking. If it's on offer, order the heavenly *polpette al ragù* (meatballs in tomato sauce). (081 42 15 33; Via Santa Teresa a Chiaia 47; meals around €16; 12.30-3.30pm daily, plus 7.30-11.30pm Fri & Sat; [M] Piazza Amedeo)

Pasticceria Mennella

PASTRIES €

10 MAP P80, C2

If you eat only one sweet treat in Naples (good luck with that!), make it Mennella's spectacular *frolla al limone*, a shortbread pastry filled with heavenly lemon cream. Just leave room for the *mignon* (bite-size) version of its *sciù* (choux pastry) with *crema di nocciola* (hazelnut cream). Before you go feeling guilty, remember that everything is free of preservatives and artificial additives. (081 42 60 26; www.pasticceriamennella.it; Via Carducci 50-52; pastries from €1.50; 6.30am-9.30pm Mon-Fri, to 10.30pm Sat, 7am-9.30pm Sun; [M] Piazza Amedeo)

Cook Like a Local

If all those smashing meals inspire the cook within, state-of-the-art cooking school **Toffini Academy** (Map p80, A3; 081 66 53 36; www.toffini.it; Via Martucci 35; 3hr cooking course from €60; [bus] 627 to Via Crispi, [M] Piazza Amedeo) runs relaxed, small-group Neapolitan cooking courses suitable for all levels. English-language options include homemade pizza making, pasta and seafood, as well as Sunday-lunch favourite *ragù napoletano*.

Dialetti

ITALIAN €€

11 MAP P80, D3

On-point Dialetti takes its cues from cities like New York, London and Sydney. You'll find a snug, vintage-pimped lounge corner at the front, a communal dining table with views of the glassed-in kitchen, and a softly lit dining room beyond it. Service is attentive and the daily-changing menu champions gorgeous ingredients, cooked beautifully and with subtle contemporary tweaks. (081 248 1158; www.facebook.com/dialettinapoli; Vico Satriano 10; meals around €32; noon-3.30pm & 6-11pm; [bus] 128, 140, 151 to Riviera di Chiaia)

Feast at a Fishmonger

Run by brothers Francesco, Gennaro and Luigi, Chiaia fishmonger **Pescheria Mattiucci** (Map p80, D3; ☎081 251 2215; www.pescheriamattiucci.com; Vico Belledonne a Chiaia 27; crudo dishes €6, cooked dishes €10-12; ⏲12.30-3pm & 6.30-11pm Tue-Sat; 🚌E6 to Piazza dei Martiri, Ⓜ Piazza Amedeo) transforms daily into an intimate, sociable seafood eatery. Perch yourself on a bar stool, order a vino, and watch the team prepare your tapas-style *crudo* to order. You'll also find a number of simple, beautifully cooked seafood dishes. For the best experience, go early in the week, when the crowds are thin and the ambience much more relaxed.

Officina del Mare

SEAFOOD **€€**

12 MAP P80, G5

While this place lacks the waterfront views of its neighbours, it also lacks the dated kitsch. Furthermore, both the chef and sommelier hail from Naples' illustrious Grand Hotel Parker's, translating into gracious service and beautifully prepared dishes made with top-notch seafood. Top choices include the *crudo,* pasta (most notably the *scialatiello* with seafood) and the grilled fish mains. (☎081 1935 3543; Piazzetta Marinari 20-21; meals around €40; ⏲11.30am-11.30pm; 🚌128, E6 to Via Santa Lucia)

Trattoria Castel dell'Ovo

SEAFOOD **€€**

13 MAP P80, G5

Many locals ditch the bigger, more touristy restaurants situated on Borgo Marinaro for this cheaper, friendlier bolthole. Sit beside bobbing boats and tuck into surf staples such as *zuppa di pesce* (fish soup) and *insalata di polipo* (octopus salad with fresh tomato). Even if it's not on the menu, it's worth requesting the spaghetti with prawns, mussels, zucchini and *parmigiano reggiano*. Cash only accepted. (☎081 764 63 52; Via Luculliana 28; meals €25; ⏲8-11pm Fri-Wed Jul-Sep, 1-3.15pm & 8-11pm Mon-Wed, Fri & Sat, 1-3.15pm Sun Oct-Jun; 🚌128 to Via Santa Lucia)

Ristorantino dell'Avvocato

NEAPOLITAN **€€€**

14 MAP P80, G4

This elegant yet welcoming restaurant is a favourite of Neapolitan gastronomes. Apple of their eye is affable lawyer turned head chef Raffaele Cardillo, whose passion for Campania's culinary heritage merges with a knack for subtle, refreshing twists – think coffee papardelle served with mullet *ragù*. (☎081 032 00 47; www.ilristorantinodellavvocato.it; Via Santa Lucia 115-117;

meals €40-45; noon-3pm daily, plus 7-11pm Tue-Sat; ; 128, E6 to Via Santa Lucia)

Da Ettore

NEAPOLITAN, PIZZA **€€**

15 MAP P80, G4

Its name in green neon, this wood-panelled octogenarian celebrates tradition with quick-witted veteran waiters, faithful regulars and a roaming Neapolitan busker. The *genovese* (pasta with slow-cooked onion) here is legendary, with other notable options including the barbecued meats and the *pagnottiello,* pizza dough filled with the likes of *parmigiana di melanzane* (aubergine parmigiana). (081 764 0498; www.facebook.com/ristopizzaettore; Via Santa Lucia 56; pizza from €6, meals €20-€35; 12.30-3.30pm & 7pm-midnight Mon-Sat; 128, E6 to Via Santa Lucia)

Drinking

L'Antiquario

COCKTAIL BAR

16 MAP P80, E4

If you take your cocktails seriously, slip into this sultry, speakeasy-inspired den. Wrapped in art nouveau wallpaper, it's the domain of Neapolitan barkeep Alex Frezza, a finalist at the 2014 Bombay Sapphire World's Most Imaginative Bartender Awards. Straddling classic and contemporary, the drinks are impeccable, made with passion and meticulous attention to detail. Live jazz-centric tunes add to the magic on Wednesdays. (081 764 53 90; www.facebook.com/antiquarionapoli; Via Gaetani 2; 7.30pm-2.30am; 151, 154 to Piazza Vittoria)

Barril

BAR

17  MAP P80, D3

From street level, stairs lead down to this softly lit, buzzing garden bar, where grown-up, fashionable types mingle among birdcage seats and vintage Cinzano posters. Fresh, competent cocktails include giant, creamy piña coladas, and there's a dedicated gin list with numerous tonic waters for a customised G&T. Bites include cheese and charcuterie platters, plus a decent selection of complimentary *aperitivo*-time snacks. (393 9814362; www.barril.it; Via G Fiorelli 11; 7pm-2am Tue-Sun; ; M Piazza Amedeo)

Ba-Bar

BAR

18  MAP P80, D3

Swinging, candlelit Ba-Bar is a solid all-rounder, punctuated with quirky vintage objects and pulling a friendly, mixed crowd. It's a top spot for a pre-dinner *aperitivo,* a lingering catch-up in the cosy back room, or a foosball game in the basement. Cocktails are well mixed, and there's a rotating list of interesting Italian wines, as well as local and foreign beers. (081 764 35 25; www.ba-bar.it; Via Bisignano 20; 5pm-2am Mon & Sun, 11am-3.30pm & 5pm-2am Tue & Wed, 11am-3.30pm & 5pm-3am Thu-Sat; ; E6 to Piazza dei Martiri)

Appetite-Piquing Aperitivo

Pre-dinner *aperitivo* is a popular ritual in Naples and Chiaia is its heartland. You'll find popular bars on and around Via Bisignano, Vico II Alabardieri, Via Alabardieri and Via Ferrigni. While some spots offer little more than a bowl of potato chips with your drink, other bars provide more appetising or substantial morsels to graze on. Among these standouts are the justifiably popular Cantine Sociali, Ba-Bar (p87) and, a little further west, Barril (p87).

Cantine Sociali

BAR

19 MAP P80, E2

Cantine Sociali is hugely popular, drawing a stylish, mixed-age crowd to its timber deck each night. The wine list is extensive and competent (if not especially cheap), the cocktails well mixed, and the free *aperitivo* buffet a satisfying spread that usually includes couscous, vegetables and *pizzette* (small pizzas). (338 3511375; www.facebook.com/cantinesocialinapoli; Piazza Giulio Rodinò 28; 6pm-2am Mon-Wed, to 3am Thu-Sun; E6 to Piazza dei Martiri)

Al Barcadero

CAFE

20 MAP P80, G5

Turn left down the steps as you walk towards Borgo Marinaro and you'll find this unpretentious waterfront bar. Plonk yourself by the water and gaze out at boat-rowing fishers and a menacing Mt Vesuvius while sipping a notoriously strong negroni. (334 1790987; Banchina Santa Lucia 2; 8am-2am Tue-Sun May-Oct, to 8pm Tue-Sun Nov-Apr; 128, E6 to Via Santa Lucia)

Entertainment

Associazione Scarlatti

CLASSICAL MUSIC

21 MAP P80, E3

Naples' premier classical-music association organises chamber-music concerts in venues that include the Museo Diocesano di Napoli. Local talent mixes it with foreign guests, which have included the Amsterdam Baroque Orchestra, St Petersburg's Mariinsky Theatre Orchestra and Belgian composer Philippe Herreweghe. (081 40 60 11; www.associazionescarlatti.it; Piazza dei Martiri 58; E6 to Piazza dei Martiri)

Shopping

Asad Ventrella: Contemporastudio

JEWELLERY

22 MAP P80, B2

Asad Ventrella is one of Naples' most respected names in jewellery design, producing statement-making wearables that are equally playful, experimental and stylish. The labyrinth is a recurring motif, as is Mediterranean mythology, underscoring objects that include rings, necklaces, bracelets and

Via Chiaia

money clips. Quirkier pieces include a pasta-shaped necklace made of solid silver. These are whimsical, confident creations with a strong sense of place. (☎081 247 99 37; www.asadventrella.it; Via Crispi 50; ⏰10am-1.30pm & 4-7.30pm Mon-Fri, 10am-1.30pm Sat; Ⓜ Piazza Amedeo)

Mattana Design JEWELLERY

23 MAP P80, B2

Pimp your fingers, wrists or neckline with Mattana's meticulously detailed creations for men and women. The studio's DNapoli line is especially intriguing, taking its inspiration from ancient Neapolitan history, mythology and culture, whether it be sirens and saints, or traditional playing cards. (☎081 66 88 31; www.mattanadesign.com; Via Crispi 24; ⏰10am-2pm & 4.30-7.30pm Mon-Sat; Ⓜ Piazza Amedeo)

Livio De Simone FASHION & ACCESSORIES

24 MAP P80, E3

The late Livio De Simone put Capri on the catwalk, dressing Audrey Hepburn and Jackie O in his bold, colourful creations. Inspired by the island, summer and the sea, his daughter, Benedetta, keeps the vision alive with the label's distinctive hand- and block-printed *robe chemesiers* (shirt dresses), frocks, suits, coats, and matching bags, purses, luggage tags, cushion covers and bowls. (☎081 764 38 27; www.liviodesimone.com; Via Domenico Morelli 17; ⏰10am-1.30pm & 4.30-8pm Mon-Sat; 🚌E6 to Piazza dei Martiri)

Walking Tour

Mergellina

Immortalised in countless lyrics, prose and paintings, bayside Mergellina is deeply etched in the city's collective memory. A place of sunbathing felines and weathered fisherfolk, it's also a neighbourhood of easy-to-miss treasures, from a cult-status Neapolitan lunch spot to long-forgotten backstreets strung with washing and the curious glances of its salt-of-the-earth residents.

Getting There

140, 151 to Riviera di Chiaia

M Mergellina (Line 2)

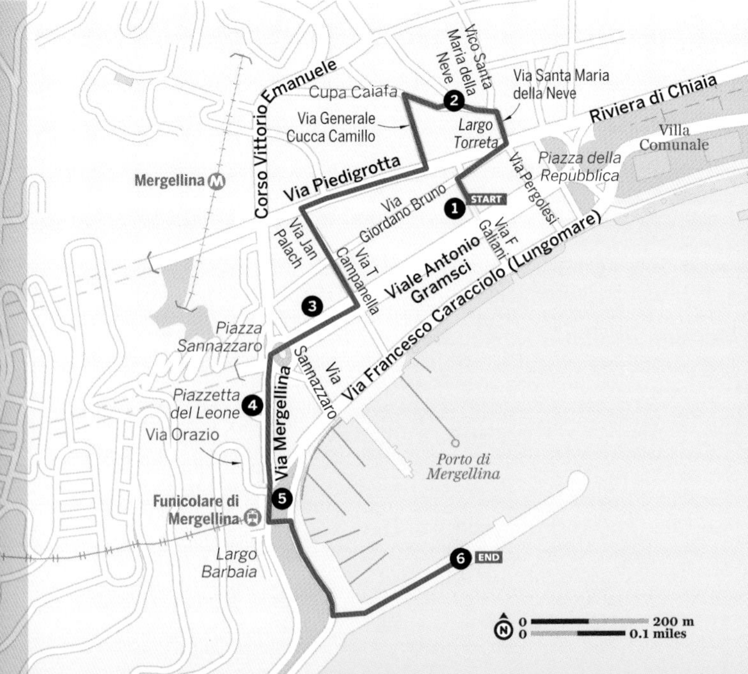

❶ Cibi Cotti

Nonna Anna may have gone to the great kitchen in the sky, but her loud, tiled lunch spot kicks on. Hidden in a market arcade, **Cibi Cotti** (☎081 68 28 44; www.facebook.com/cibicottinonnaanna; Via Galiani 30; meals €8; ⏲noon-3pm Mon-Sat) serves simple, cheap Neapolitan home-cooking; the legume dishes and *ragù* (meat and tomato sauce) are especially popular. Order at the counter and watch for a table; staffer Enzo speaks English.

❷ La Torretta di Mergellina

Mergellina's broad boulevards seem a world away from **La Torretta di Mergellina**, a tiny warren of streets where local fishers once lived. From Via Piedigrotta, enter the quarter from Via Santa Maria della Neve (which becomes Cupa Caiafa), a skinny street flanked by religious shrines, hung washing and curious locals. Turn left into Via Generale Cucca Camillo to return to Via Piedigrotta.

❸ Anna Matuozzo

Sartorialists know all about **Anna Matuozzo** (☎081 66 38 74; www.annamatuozzo.com; Viale Gramsci 26). From an apartment on Viale Gramsci, the *signora* and her daughters measure dapper gents for exquisitely hand-stitched shirts. The atelier also sells justifiably expensive silk ties and boxers, plus linen pyjamas. Call ahead.

❹ Piazzetta del Leone

The battered-looking lion in **Piazzetta del Leone** once stood by a long-gone local date tree *(dattero),* so famous that it named nearby Vico Dattero. The street itself was known as the Neapolitan Montmartre, a popular haunt for the city's 19th-century painters. The lion was moved to its current location in the 1860s, from where it still eyes up passersby.

❺ Chalet Ciro Mergellina

On weekends, locals double- and triple-park outside **Chalet Ciro Mergellina** (☎081 66 99 28; www.chaletciro.it; Via Caracciolo; gelato from €2.50, cono graffa €5; ⏲6.45am-2.30am Mon, Tue, Thu & Sun, to 3am Fri, to 4am Sat), a retro seafront chalet famous for its *graffe* (doughnuts) and gelato. If you can't decide between them, order Ciro's *cono graffa,* gelato in a doughnut cone that Neapolitans call a *bomba* (bomb).

❻ Molo Luise

Chalet Ciro fronts the Porto di Mergellina (Port of Mergellina), filled with sun-bleached fishing boats and gleaming yachts. Grab some *taralli caldi* (warm, pretzel-like biscuits) from the kerbside kiosks and stroll down the **Molo Luise**, the hulking pier that guards the marina. The view of the Castel dell'Ovo and Mt Vesuvius is especially beautiful in the late-afternoon sun.

Worth a Trip

Discover Pompeii

The ruins of Pompeii are a veritable time machine, hurling visitors back to the age of emperors and Latin chatter. Here, time remains paused at 79 AD, the city's frescoed homes, businesses and baths still waiting for their occupants to return. Few archaeological sites offer such an intimate connection to the past, and few are as deeply haunting and evocative.

www.pompeiisites.org

adult/reduced €15/9

9am-7.30pm, last entry 6pm Apr-Oct, 8.30am-5.30pm, last entry 3.30pm Nov-Mar

Circumvesuviana to Pompei Scavi–Villa dei Misteri

Villa dei Misteri

Located at the northwestern extreme of the site, this remarkably intact villa houses extraordinary wall paintings, impressive for both their scale and vivid hues. The most important of these works is the Dionysiac frieze, one of the largest and most arresting artworks from antiquity. Spanning the walls of a large dining room, the painting depicts the initiation of a bride-to-be into the cult of Dionysus, the Greek god of wine. The initiation ritual associated with the cult (known as the Dionysian Mysteries) was shrouded in secrecy, though wild rumours about sexual depravity, cruelty and social disorder led the Roman Senate to issue a decree against it in 186 BC.

Foro & Around

The Foro (Forum) was Pompeii's downtown hub, home to top-tier temples, civic institutions and important commercial activity. Before construction of the Anfiteatro, it was also the venue for gladiatorial games. At its northern end is what remains of the 2nd-century BC Tempio di Giove (Temple of Jupiter), dedicated to Jupiter, Juno and Minerva and, in its heyday, the main religious building in the city. To the right is the 2nd-century BC Macellum (market), where faded food-themed frescoes survive. To the left, the Granai del Foro houses ancient amphorae and body casts, while the southwest corner of the Forum flanks the Basilica, the 2nd-century BC seat of Pompeii's law courts and exchange. Their semicircular apses would later influence the design of early Christian churches. Just to the west of the Forum lies the Tempio di Apollo, the oldest and most important of Pompeii's religious buildings.

Terme Stabiane

These 2nd-century BC baths are the largest and best preserved in Pompeii, their original

★ Top Tips

- Buy your ticket online to avoid queues.
- There are free lockers by the entrance to the ruins.
- If you've purchased an ArteCard, make the ruins one of the first three sights you visit to enjoy free entry.
- South of the ruins, Spartacus Camping on Via Plinio offers cheap all-day parking (€5).

Take a Break

- An on-site cafeteria just north of the Foro (Forum) serves acceptable, if unremarkable, *panini*, pizza slices, salads, ice cream and other snacks.
- For a memorable lunch or dinner, make reservations at Pompeii's good-value, Michelin-starred **President** (081 850 72 45; www.ristorantepresident.it; Piazza Schettini 12; meals from €40, tasting menus €65-90; noon-3.30pm & 7pm-late Tue-Sun).

features including stuccoed ceilings. The entrance on Via dell'Abbondanza leads to the *palestra*, a sweeping, colonnaded courtyard used by training athletes. From the right side of the colonnade one enters the *apodyterium* (changing room), itself leading to the *tepidarium* (tepid bath). To the left of it is the *frigidarium* (cold bath), while to the right is the *calidarium* (hot bath). Note the hollow floors, which allowed hot air to flow through the complex from the *praefurnium*, a furnace operated by a slave. Entry to the less-impressive women's section was from Via Lupanare.

Casa del Poeta Tragico

The 1st-century AD House of the Tragic Poet is famous for its canine-themed floor mosaic, inscribed with the words *cave canem* (beware of the dog). Adorning the entrance to the house, it is one of the best-preserved mosaics at the ruins. The home is now accessed from a side entrance, which leads directly into the garden, framed by colonnades on three sides. From here, the atrium and *tablinum* (reception/living room) are visible, both of which featured beautiful mosaics. A side corridor allowed slaves to move discreetly between the atrium and the back of the house without passing through the *tablinum*. The house itself is featured in Edward Bulwer-Lytton's 19th-century novel *The Last Days of Pompeii*.

Casa del Fauno

The largest and wealthiest private abode in Pompeii is named after the delicate bronze statue of the *Faun* (in reality the god Pan) in the *impluvium*, a shallow rectangular pool in the atrium. The statue is a copy of the original, which is now housed in Naples' Museo Archeologico Nazionale. The smaller rooms to the sides off the atrium were most likely bedrooms or sitting rooms, while the room at the back was the *tablinum*, used by the owner to discuss business with clients. The property features two atria (most homes had one). The smaller of the two reveals the remnants of a WWII Allied bomb in its southeast corner. A communicating room between the first and second peristyles (colonnaded courtyards) features a copy of a mosaic depicting Alexander the Great warring against the Persian king Darius III. Considered the best-known depiction of the ancient Greek king, the original is now also housed in Naples' archaeological museum.

Casa dei Vettii

The House of the Vettii is celebrated for its vivid frescoes, while its peristyle still includes original marble decoration. The most famous of its frescoes is a depiction of Priapus, his gigantic phallus balanced on a pair of scales. Roman god of fertility and the protector of horticulture and viticulture, his portrayal symbolised the success of the property's sibling owners, former slaves or freedmen who made their fortune selling wine and agricultural products.

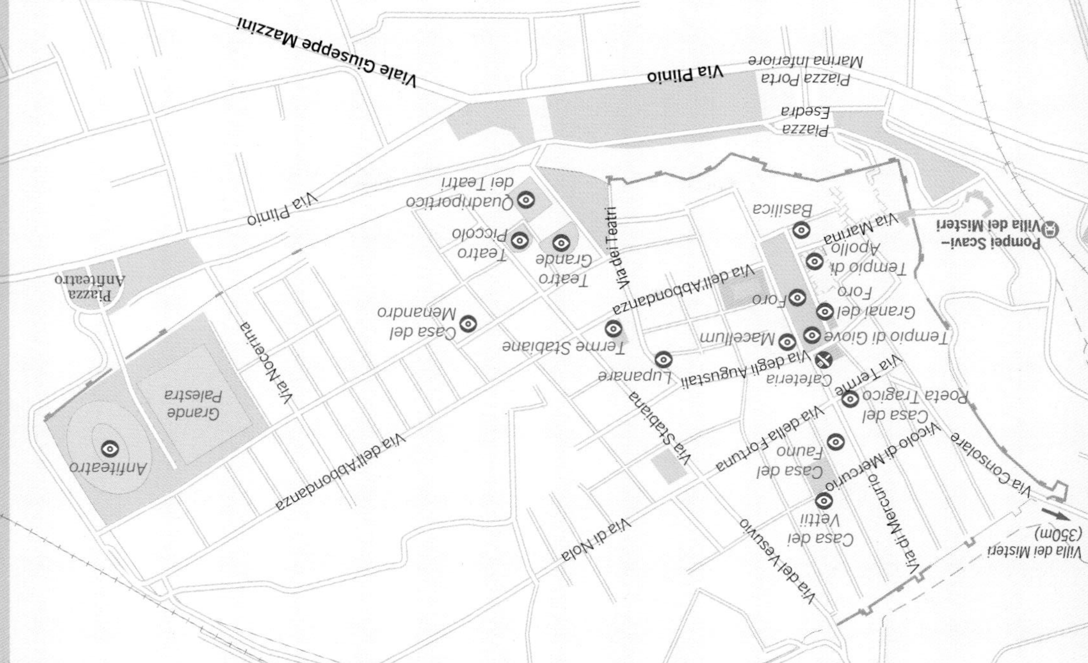
Anfiteatro
Grande Palestra
Piazza Anfiteatro
Via Nocerina
Via dell'Abbondanza
Via Plinio
Viale Giuseppe Mazzini
Casa del Menandro
Teatro Piccolo
Quadriportico dei Teatri
Teatro Grande
Terme Stabiane
Via dei Teatri
Via dell'Abbondanza
Lupanare
Via Stabiana
Via di Nola
Via Plinio
Piazza Porta Marina Inferiore
Piazza Esedra
Basilica
Via Marina
Tempio di Apollo
Foro
Granai del Foro
Tempio di Giove
Macellum
Via degli Augustali
Cafeteria
Via Terme
Casa del Poeta Tragico
Via della Fortuna
Casa del Fauno
Vicolo di Mercurio
Casa dei Vettii
Via di Mercurio
Via del Vesuvio
Via Consolare
Villa dei Misteri (350m)
Pompei Scavi–Villa dei Misteri

Twelve frescoes depict mythological scenes, among them the condemnation of a naked Lapith King Ixion for betraying Zeus, the murder of Theban king Pentheus by the female followers of Dionysus, and a brawny infant Hercules strangling snakes.

Casa del Menandro

In the right-hand corner of this upmarket home's frescoed atrium is a *lararium,* a shrine dedicated to the guardian spirits of a Roman household. The atrium leads into a room depicting Cassandra, the Trojan Horse and Laocoön from Homer's epic poem *Iliad,* while the peristyle is one of the best preserved in Pompeii. A doorway on the right side of the peristyle leads to a private bathhouse, while the central *exhedra* (recess) at the far end of the peristyle features a striking fresco of the ancient Greek dramatist Menander.

Lupanare

Pompeii's most salacious building, the Lupanare brothel inhabits an area once known as a red-light district. The explicit wall frescoes were an enticement of sorts for clients, who were subsequently 'entertained' in one of the five rooms on the ground floor. Each room featured a stone bed and latrine, and the walls remain etched with the graffiti of its sex workers. That this graffiti is in various languages is telling: most prostitutes were slaves or former slaves. The 1st floor harbours another five rooms, assumed to be the sleeping quarters of the workers and the brothel's owner.

Teatro Grande

JAVEN/SHUTTERSTOCK ©

Pompeii: A Primer

The origins of Pompeii are uncertain, though it seems likely that it was founded in the 7th century BC by the Campanian Oscans. Over the next seven centuries the city fell to the Greeks and the Samnites before becoming a Roman city in 80 BC.

As terrible as the volcanic eruption of 79 AD was, it could have been worse. Seventeen years earlier Pompeii had been devastated by an earthquake and much of the 20,000-strong population had been evacuated. Many had not returned by the time Vesuvius blew, although 2000 denizens perished nonetheless.

From an archaeological point of view, Pompeii is priceless. Much of its value lies in the fact that it wasn't simply blown away by Vesuvius in 79 AD, nor left abandoned or transformed over the centuries. Instead, it was buried under a layer of *lapilli* (burning fragments of pumice stone), forever snap-locking the city in the 1st century AD.

The Theatres

Pompeii's 'theatre district' includes the 2nd-century BC Teatro Grande (Large Theatre). Carved into the lava mass on which Pompeii was originally built, the outdoor arena was able to seat 5000 spectators. The venue was restored in the 1st century BC by architect M. Artorius M. L. Primus, whose signature remains visible at the entrance to the eastern corridor. Also dating from the 1st century BC is the adjoining Teatro Piccolo (also known as the Odeon), formerly roofed and known for its impressive acoustics. Behind the Teatro Grande's stage, the porticoed Quadriportico dei Teatri was originally used by audiences as a place to stroll between acts before becoming a barracks for gladiators. Inscriptions recording their successes in gladiatorial games were found on its columns, as was a collection of helmets, shields, daggers and leg guards, mostly now stored in Naples' Museo Archeologico Nazionale.

Anfiteatro

The Anfiteatro is the oldest known Roman amphitheatre in existence. Dating from 70 BC, its spectacles thrilled up to 20,000 guests at a time. These included battles between gladiators, as well as between men and animals. Passions boiled over in 59 AD, when rival spectators from Pompeii and Nucera fought in violent clashes, immortalised in a fresco now displayed in Naples' Museo Archeologico Nazionale. The riot led the Senate to impose a decade-long ban on games in Pompeii, revoked three years later after the major earthquake of 62 AD.

Worth a Trip

Explore Mt Vesuvius

Like all bad boys, Mt Vesuvius radiates a fatalistic magnetism. The only active volcano on mainland Europe, its silence belies a power so great that it holds the lives of millions in the balance. While most visitors head straight for its panoramic summit, Vesuvius' fertile slopes are a lesser-known pleasure, laced with walking trails at odds with the volcano's menacing reputation.

crater adult/reduced €10/8

crater 9am-6pm Jul & Aug, to 5pm Apr-Jun & Sep, to 4pm Mar & Oct, to 3pm Nov-Feb, ticket office closes 1hr before crater

Gran Cono

Reaching Mt Vesuvius' Gran Cono (Great Cone) is a literal and figurative high. The summit crater – 230m deep and 650m in diameter – sits 1282m above sea level, offering a breath-taking panorama that (on a clear day) takes in Naples, the Campi Flegrei and the bay islands. One can also eyeball the Monti Picentini, part of the Apennine Mountains that run down the Italian peninsula. Buses reach the summit car park and ticket office, from where an 860m gravel path leads up to the summit. If arriving by car, the car park is further down the slope but serviced by a shuttle bus (return trip €2). Admission to the summit includes a free guided walk half-way around the crater.

Parco Nazionale del Vesuvio

Mt Vesuvius is the focal point of the **Parco Nazionale del Vesuvio** (Vesuvius National Park; www.epnv.it), a national park covering 8482 protected hectares. Its rich fauna includes around 140 species of birds, including hawks and imperial ravens. The volcano's dual summit provides diversity of flora as well, with classic Mediterranean vegetation on rockier Vesuvius proper and a mix of chestnuts, maples and holm oaks on the cooler north-facing slopes of Mt Somma. Nine marked nature trails trace the park, varying in length and difficulty, from the easy 'Vallone della Profica' (1.7km) to the challenging 'Along the Cognoli' (8km). The best route for reaching the crater is the moderately difficult 'Gran Cono' (3.8km). Alternatively, **Horse Riding Tour Naples** (☎345 8560306; www.horseridingnaples.com; guided tour €60) runs daily morning and afternoon horse-riding tours of the park, weather permitting. Tours include transfers to/from Naples, Pompeii and Ercolano (Herculaneum).

★ Top Tips

- Head up on a clear day for guaranteed views.
- Wear comfortable trainers or trekking shoes, and bring a warm top as the summit can feel chilly, even in summer.
- If driving up, arrive early to avoid long queues for a parking spot (€5).
- If arriving by bus, the public **EAV** (☎800 211388; www.eavsrl.it) bus service from Pompeii is cheaper than the private shuttles and drops you off at the same point. Ignore touts in Pompeii telling you that the public bus isn't running that day.

✕ Take a Break

- Snacks and drinks can be purchased by the summit ticket office.
- For quality wine and food, head back down to Ercolano and settle in at Viva Lo Re (p101).

Worth a Trip

Uncover Herculaneum (Ercolano)

Overshadowed by Pompeii, Herculaneum would elsewhere be the star of the show. Buried for centuries under volcanic mud, its ancient homes, shops and public spaces offer instant, vivid access to Roman times. Littered with everything from carbonised furniture and shelves to plunge pools and dining-room frescoes, its treasures are remarkable and revealing, thinning the line between past and present.

081 857 53 47

www.coopculture.it

Corso Resina 187, Ercolano

adult/reduced €11/5.50

8.30am-7.30pm Apr-Oct, to 5pm Nov-Mar

Circumvesuviana to Ercolano–Scavi

Casa dello Scheletro

Named for the human bones found on the upper floor during 19th-century excavations, the House of the Skeleton is actually made up of three adjoining houses, the middle of which features a covered atrium. The building features five styles of mosaic flooring, as well as the remnants of a security grill that once covered a skylight. Of the house's mythically themed wall mosaics, only the faded ones are originals; the others are now housed in Naples' Museo Archeologico Nazionale.

Terme Maschili

The Men's Baths formed part of the Terme del Foro (Forum Baths), which included a separate female bathing area. Note the ancient latrine to the left of the entrance before stepping into the *apodyterium* (changing room). To the left of the changing room is the domed *frigidarium* (cold bath), which was actually the last room involved in the bathing process, used after the warmer pools. These are found to the right of the changing room. First is the *tepadarium* (tepid bath), its sunken floor mosaic of the sea god Triton evidence of the seismic activity that shook the area before Mt Vesuvius' catastrophic eruption. From the *tepadarium* one reaches the apsidal *caldarium* (hot bath).

Sede degli Augustali

The central cell of the Hall of the Augustals harbours some of the best-preserved frescoes in Herculaneum. Adorning the left wall is a depiction of ancient hero Hercules about to enter Mt Olympus, accompanied by the Roman goddesses Juno and Minerva and, in the form of a rainbow, Jupiter, considered king of gods. The fresco directly opposite depicts Hercules and horned divinity Achelous, who famously battled it out over the river nymph Deianira.

★ Top Tips

- Wear a hat, sunscreen and comfortable, flat shoes.
- If you've purchased an ArteCard, make Herculaneum one of the first three sights you visit to enjoy free entry.
- Never use flash photography.

Take a Break

- The site includes a self-service cafe, with vending machines selling snacks, water, soft drinks and coffee.
- For beautiful regional dishes or a simple glass of well-chosen wine, settle in at genteel **Viva Lo Re** (☎081 739 02 07; www.vivalore.it; Corso Resina 261, Ercolano; meals €32; noon-3.30pm & 7.30-11.30pm Tue-Sat, noon-3.30pm Sun; wifi).

Decumano Massimo

Herculaneum's ancient high street is lined with shops, and fragments of advertisements. Seek out the so-called Cucumas Shop, where a fresco depicts four pitchers in different colours, each symbolising a particular libation and its price per weight. The figure hovering above them is Semo Sancus, a divinity worshipped by the Sabines, Umbrians and Romans, and considered a protector of businesses. Further east along the street, a crucifix found in an upstairs room of the Casa del Bicentenario (Bicentenary House) provides possible evidence of a Christian presence in pre-Vesuvius Herculaneum.

Casa di Nettuno e Anfitrite

The aristocratic House of Neptune and Amphitrite is one of the most celebrated in Herculaneum. Believed to be the home of a wealthy, art-loving merchant, it takes its name from the extraordinary glass-paste wall mosaic adorning the *triclinium* (dining room), depicting the ancient sea god and his nymph bride. Perpendicular to this mosaic is a *nymphaeum* (fountain and bath as a shrine to the water nymph), itself decorated with colourful, hunting-themed mosaics. The warm, rich colours hint at how lavish the original interior must have been. Annexed to the house is an impressively preserved food store, complete with wooden shelves and terracotta amphorae.

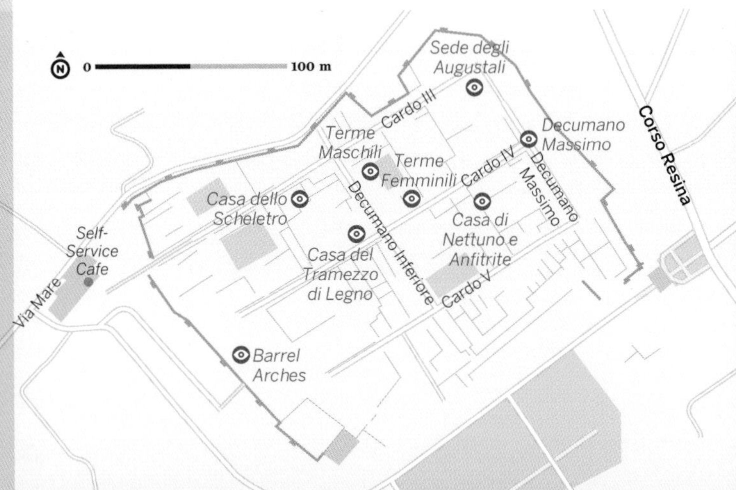

Herculaneum: From Past to Present

In contrast to modern Ercolano, an uninspiring Neapolitan suburb 12km south of Naples proper, ancient Herculaneum was a peaceful fishing and port town of about 4000 inhabitants. It was also something of a resort for wealthy Romans and Campanians. Its fate runs parallel to that of Pompeii. Destroyed by an earthquake in 62 AD, its proximity to Mt Vesuvius saw it submerged in a 16m-thick sea of mud during the volcano's eruption in 79 AD. The fossilised settlement itself was rediscovered in 1709 and amateur excavations were carried out intermittently until 1874, with many finds carted off to Naples to decorate the houses of the well-to-do or ending up in museums. Serious archaeological work began again in 1927 and continues to this day. It's a slow-going process, with much of the ancient site buried beneath the concrete jungle of modern Ercolano. Indeed, note that at any given time some of Herculaneum's time-stuck treasures will invariably be shut for restoration.

Terme Femminili

Cardo IV is home to the women's section of the Terme del Foro (Forum Baths), the Terme Femminili. Though smaller than its male counterpart, it boasts finer floor mosaics. These include a vivid depiction of the muscular Triton in the barrel-vaulted *apodyterium*, which also features storage shelves for bathers. The next room was the *tepidarium*, itself followed by the *caldarium*. Beyond it is the service area, with a well and furnace used to service both the women's and men's sections of the complex.

Casa del Tramezzo di Legno

The House of the Wooden Partition is named for the well-preserved wooden screen which divides the atrium from the *tablinum*, where the owner would talk business with his clients. Rings and supports on the screen's panels would have once supported oil lamps. Unusually, the house features two atria, which likely belonged to two separate dwellings that were merged in the 1st century AD.

Barrel Arches

The horror of the 79 AD eruption is dramatically captured at the Barrel Arches, a row of vaulted rooms that once flanked the shore. Originally used to store boats and other goods, they are filled with the skeletons of dying locals, many of whom had fled to the beach only to be overcome by the infernal heat of clouds surging down from Vesuvius. In total, 333 skeletons were discovered here by a team of archaeologists in the early 1980s. Incredibly, the volcanic deposits pushed the shoreline out several hundreds of metres.

Worth a Trip

Marvel at the Reggia di Caserta

The largest royal palace in the world by volume, the Reggia di Caserta is also one of its most beautiful. Commissioned by Charles VII after liberating Naples and Sicily from the Austrians, its frescoed, silk-lined rooms and spectacular baroque gardens attest to the riches of the Bourbon dynasty and the bold, brilliant ambition of its founding architect, Luigi Vanvitelli.

Palazzo Reale

www.reggiadicaserta.beniculturali.it

Viale Douhet 22, Caserta

adult/reduced €12/6

palace 8.30am-7.30pm Wed-Mon, reduced hours rest of year

Caserta

The Palace

Home to four courtyards, 1200 rooms and 1790 windows, the Reggia is quite simply epic. From the central octagonal vestibule, Vanvitelli's monumental Staircase of Honour leads up to Royal Apartments. Crowning the Alexander Room is Mariano Rossi's spectacular vault fresco, the *Marriage of Alexander the Great and Roxane.* Further along, the back rooms off the Room of Astraea house historic wooden models of the Reggia, along with architectural drawings and early sketches by Luigi Vanvitelli and his son, Carlo. The stuccoed Throne Room incorporates portraits of Naples' sovereign rules, while the Rooms of the Seasons delight with historical and landscape paintings, allegorical frescoes, and precious ceramics from Naples' Capodimonte. Kind Ferdinand II breathed his last breath in the King's Bedroom, beyond which lies the beautifully appointed Queen's Apartment and the Palatine Library, renowned for its collection of Neapolitan opera, ballet and music *libretti*.

Parco Reale

Inspired by Versailles in France and the Royal Palace of La Granja de San Ildefonso in Spain, the Royal Park is equally monumental. Just north of the palace building, to the left, is the Bosco Vecchio (Old Forest), home to the Peschiera Grande lake and the Castelluccia – a miniature fortified castle, transformed in the 19th century into a post-hunting rest spot for royal guests. The park's spectacular centrepiece is the Via d'Acqua, a row of basins and mythologically themed fountains that stretch up to a waterfall. Beside it lies the fabled Giardino Inglese (English Garden), commissioned by Maria Carolina of Austria and realised by Carlo Vanvitelli and English gardener John Andrew Graefer.

★ Top Tips

- Bicycle hire is available at the back of the palace building: choose between a standard model (€4), electric bike (€4) or tandem (€7).
- For a lazy overview of the grounds, pony-and-trap rides are available for the set price of €50 for a 40-minute ride (up to five people).

Take a Break

- Coffee, sandwiches and snacks can be purchased at the palace cafe, located on the ground floor at the northern end.
- An altogether better-quality option is cafe **Martucci** (☎0823 32 08 03; www.facebook.com/martucci.caffe; Via Roma 9, Caserta; pastries from €1.50, sandwiches from €3.50, salads €7.50; 5am-10.30pm;), located 250m east of the Reggia.

Explore

Capri Town & the Isle of Capri

Capri is beautiful – seriously beautiful. Steep cliffs rise majestically from an impossibly blue sea and elegant villas drip with wisteria and bougainvillea. The island's main town is Capri Town, its tiny, car-free streets lined with whitewashed stone buildings, elegant restaurants and high-end boutiques. Beyond them, trails lead everywhere from ancient ruins to sublime vistas.

Ferries dock at Marina Grande, from where tour boats depart for the dazzling Grotta Azzurra (p115). To reach Capri Town (p114), catch the panoramic funicular. In Capri Town, the funicular stop is steps away from Piazza Umberto I (p114), the town's see-and-be-seen epicentre. From the square, Via Le Botteghe (which becomes Via Croce and, further along, Via Tiberio) shoots towards Villa Jovis (p109), a beautiful 2.2km walk to the northeast. From Villa Jovis, a panoramic trail leads to Villa Lysis (p109). To reach Villa San Michele di Axel Munthe (p111), catch a local bus from Capri Town to Anacapri.

Getting There & Around

Year-round ferry services run to/from Naples and Sorrento. Seasonal routes include Ischia and the Amalfi Coast.

Runs between Marina Grande and Capri Town. The ticket booth in Marina Grande is behind the tourist office on the harbour.

Autobus ATC runs buses between Marina Grande, Capri Town, Marina Piccola and Anacapri.

Capri Town & the Isle of Capri Map on p112

Isle of Capri S-F/SHUTTERSTOCK ©

Top Experience

Retreat to the Capri Villas

From scandal-riddled Roman emperors and shamed French poets to an enlightened Swedish medic, Capri's high-profile residents have helped shape and solidify the island's mythology, legend and intrigue. And while they may come and go, their stories, passions and legacies live on in the evocative villas they once called home.

Villa Lysis

A 40-minute walk from Piazza Umberto I in Capri Town is the beautifully melancholic, rarely crowded **Villa Lysis** (pictured left; Map p112, G1; www.villalysiscapri.com; Via Lo Capo 12; €2; 10am-6pm Thu-Tue summer, to 4pm Thu-Tue winter). Set on a clifftop on Capri's northeast tip, the art nouveau villa was the one-time retreat of French poet Jacques d'Adelsward-Fersen, who came to Capri in 1904 to escape a gay sex scandal in Paris. Fersen's scandal-plagued life ended in 1923 with a lethal cocaine-champagne cocktail.

Unlike other stately homes, the interior has been left almost entirely empty; this is a place to let your imagination flesh out the details. One notable curiosity is the 'Chinese room' in the basement which includes a semicircular opium den with a swastika emblazoned on the floor. Fersen became addicted to opium following a visit to Ceylon in the early 1900s; the swastika is the Sanskrit symbol for well-being. Equally transfixing is the sun-dappled garden, a triumph of classical grandiosity half given over to nature.

The €2 entry fee includes an explanatory pamphlet available in Italian and English. Afterwards, it is possible to take a steep, winding path, the Sentiero delle Calanche, to Villa Jovis (20 minutes away).

Villa Jovis

Located a 45-minute walk east of Capri Town along Via Tiberio, **Villa Jovis** (Jupiter's Villa; Map p112, H1; Via A Maiuri; adult/reduced €6/3; 10am-6pm Wed-Mon Jun-Aug, reduced hours rest of year, closed Jan–mid-Mar) was the largest and most sumptuous of 12 Roman villas commissioned by Roman Emperor Tiberius on Capri, and his main island residence. A vast complex, now reduced to ruins, it pandered to the emperor's supposedly debauched tastes, and included imperial quarters and extensive bathing areas set in dense gardens and woodland.

★ Top Tip

- If you are here between June and August, you may be able to catch one of the classical concerts that take place in the gardens of Villa San Michele di Axel Munthe. Check the website for the current program and reservation information.

Take a Break

- On the path up to Villa Jovis, down-to-earth **Lo Sfizio** (081 837 41 28; Via Tiberio 7e; pizzas €7-11, meals €28-42; noon-3pm & 7pm-midnight Wed-Mon Apr-Dec) serves typical regional dishes, from pizza and handmade pasta to grilled meats and baked fish.
- In Anacapri, local-favourite **Le Arcate** (081 837 35 88; Via de Tommaso 24; pizzas €7-11, meals €30; noon-3pm & 7pm-midnight) offers pizzas and pasta classics like *ravioli alla caprese* (pasta filled with ricotta, parmigiano reggiano and marjoram).

Celebrity Island

The first big name to decamp on Capri was Emperor Tiberius in AD 27. A man of sadistic sexual perversions, at least if the Roman author Suetonius is to be believed, he left deep scars and, until modern times, his name was equated with evil by the islanders. When the Swedish doctor Axel Munthe first began picking about the Roman ruins on the island in the early 20th century and built his villa on the site of a Tiberian palace, locals would observe that it was all *'roba di Tiberio'* – Tiberius' stuff.

The discovery of the spectacular Grotta Azzurra in 1826 helped draw artists such as John Singer Sargent, musicians including Debussy, intellectuals, industrialists and writers, attracted by the island's beauty and, in some cases, the availability of the local lads. An early habitué, Alfred Krupp, the German industrialist and arms manufacturer, was involved in a gay scandal, while author Norman Douglas set all manner of tongues wagging.

In 1905 the author Maxim Gorky moved to Capri after failing to topple the Russian tsar, and five years later Lenin stopped by for a visit. In the course of the early 20th century Chilean poet Pablo Neruda visited regularly, while British writers Compton Mackenzie and Graham Greene lived here for extended periods.

The spectacular location of Villa Jovis (pictured left) posed major headaches for Tiberius' architects. The main problem was how to collect and store enough water to supply the villa's baths and 3000-sq-metre gardens. The solution they eventually hit upon was to build a complex canal system to transport rainwater to four giant storage tanks, whose remains you can still see today.

Beside the ticket office is the 330m-high **Salto di Tiberio** (Tiberius' Leap), a sheer cliff from where, as the story goes, Tiberius had out-of-favour subjects hurled into the sea. True or not, the stunning views are real enough; if you suffer from vertigo, tread carefully.

Villa San Michele di Axel Munthe

The former home of Swedish doctor, psychiatrist and animal-rights advocate Axel Munthe, **Villa San Michele di Axel Munthe** (Map p112, D1; www.villasanmichele.eu; Via Axel Munthe 34; €8; 9am-6pm May-Sep, reduced hours rest of year) should be included on every visitor's itinerary. Built on the site of the ruins of a Roman villa, the gardens make a beautiful setting for a tranquil stroll, with pathways flanked by immaculate flowerbeds.

The villa is an easy 350m walk northeast of Piazza Vittoria in Anacapri, along Via Capodimonte (which becomes Via Axel Munthe).

A
B
C
D
1
2
3
4
5
6
Grotta Azzurra
Punta dell'Arcera
Via La Fabbrica
Traversa la Vigna
Villa San Michele di Axel Munthe
Bagno di Tiberio
Scala Fenicia
Via Grotta Azzurra
ANACAPRI
Via G Orlandi
Seggiovia (Funicular)
Via Boffe
Via de Tommaso
Via Capodimonte
Via Pagliaro
Via Caprile
Cala del Rio
Via Tuoro
Monte Cappello (514m)
Sentiero dei Fortini
Monte Santa Maria (495m)
Via Nuova del Faro
Via Migliera
Monte Solaro (589m)
Migliera (304m)
Punta di Mulo
Cala del Tombosiello
Cala Marmolata
Lido del Faro
Punta del Tuono
Punta Ventroso
Punta Carena
Tyrrhenian Sea
For reviews see
Top Experiences p108
Sights p114
Eating p115
Drinking p117
Shopping p117
0
2 km
0
1 miles

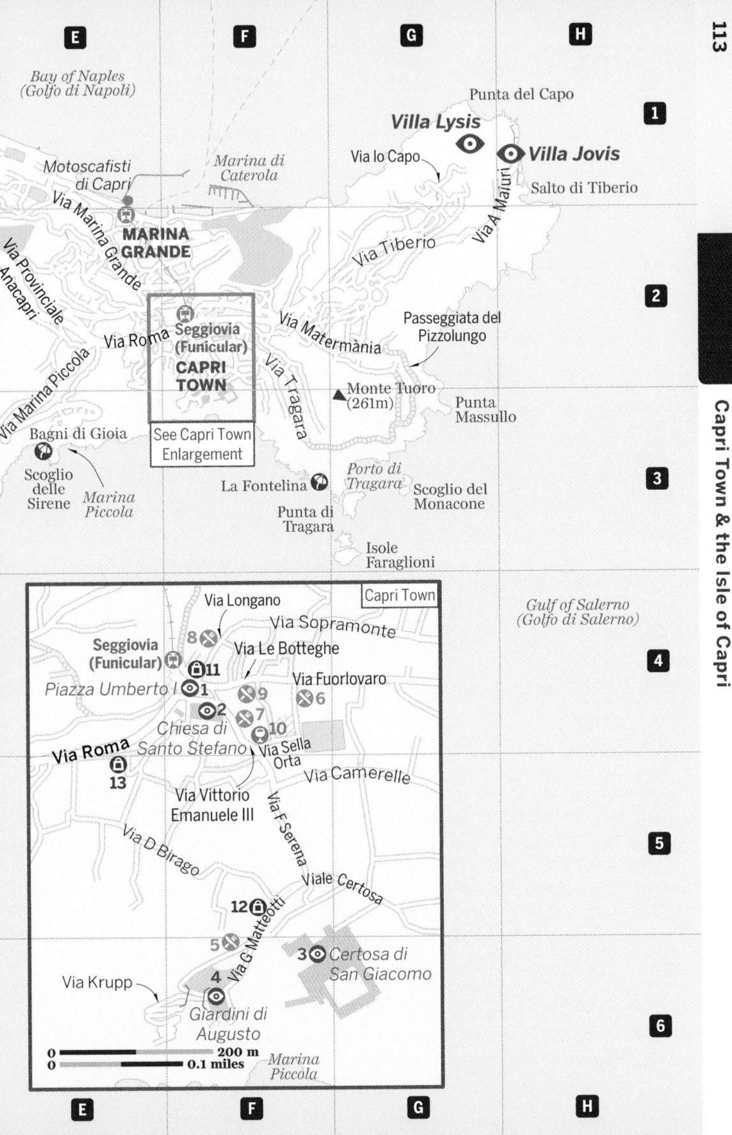
E
F
G
H
1
2
3
4
5
6
Bay of Naples
(Golfo di Napoli)
Punta del Capo
Villa Lysis
Villa Jovis
Via lo Capo
Salto di Tiberio
Motoscafisti
di Capri
Marina di
Caterola
Via Marina Grande
MARINA
GRANDE
Via Tiberio
Via A Maiuri
Via Provinciale
Anacapri
Seggiovia
(Funicular)
CAPRI
TOWN
Via Roma
Via Matermània
Passeggiata del
Pizzolungo
Via Marina Piccola
Via Tragara
Monte Tuoro
(261m)
Punta
Massullo
Bagni di Gioia
See Capri Town
Enlargement
Scoglio
delle
Sirene
Marina
Piccola
La Fontelina
Porto di
Tragara
Scoglio del
Monacone
Punta di
Tragara
Isole
Faraglioni
Capri Town
Gulf of Salerno
(Golfo di Salerno)
Via Longano
Via Sopramonte
Via Le Botteghe
Seggiovia
(Funicular)
11
8
Via Fuorlovaro
Piazza Umberto I
1
9
6
2
7
10
Chiesa di
Santo Stefano
Via Sella
Orta
Via Roma
13
Via Camerelle
Via Vittorio
Emanuele III
Via F Serena
Via D Birago
Viale Certosa
12
Via G Matteotti
5
3
Certosa di
San Giacomo
4
Via Krupp
Giardini di
Augusto
0
200 m
0
0.1 miles
Marina
Piccola
E
F
G
H

Capri Town

Sights

Piazza Umberto I PIAZZA

1 MAP P112, F4

Located beneath the 17th-century clock tower and framed by see-and-be-seen cafes, this showy, open-air salon is central to your Capri experience, especially in the evening when the main activity in these parts is dressing up and hanging out. Be prepared for the cost of the front-row seats – the moment you sit down for a drink, you're going to pay handsomely for the grandstand views (around €7 for a cappuccino and €18 for a couple of glasses of white wine).

Adorned with majolica tiles thought to date from the 18th century, the clock tower is one of Italy's most diligent, marking every quarter hour.

Chiesa di Santo Stefano CHURCH

2 MAP P112, F4

Though not remarkable in itself, Capri's main church, named after its patron saint, is a tempting haven from the bottlenecks of tourists on the streets outside. The wooden doors embellished with imitation marble date from the mid-18th century and were inspired by Villa Jovis on Capri. Note the pair of languidly reclining patricians in the chapel to the south of the main altar, who seem to mirror some of the mildly debauched folk in the cafes outside. (081 837 23 96; Piazza Umberto I; 9am-7pm summer, 10am-2pm winter)

Certosa di San Giacomo MONASTERY

3 MAP P112, F6

Founded in 1363, this substantial monastery is generally considered to be the finest remaining example of Caprese architecture and today houses a school, a library, a temporary exhibition space and a museum with some evocative 17th-century paintings. Be sure to look at the cloisters, which have a real sense of faded glory (the smaller is 14th century, the larger 16th century). To get here take Via Vittorio Emanuele III, east of Piazza Umberto I, which meanders down to the monastery. (081 837 62 18; Viale Certosa 40; adult/reduced €6/3; 10am-2pm Tue-Sun Jan-Mar, to 7pm Apr-Aug, to 5pm Sep-Dec)

Giardini di Augusto GARDENS

4 MAP P112, F6

As their name suggests, these gardens near the Certosa di San Giacomo were founded by Emperor Augustus. Rising in a series of flowered terraces, they lead to a lookout point offering breathtaking views over to the **Isole Faraglioni**, a group of three limestone stacks rising out of the sea. (Gardens of Augustus; €1; 9am-7.30pm summer, 9.30am-5.30pm winter)

Grotta Azzurra

Capri's most famous attraction is the **Grotta Azzurra** (Blue Grotto; Map p112, B1; €14; ⏲9am-5pm), an unusual sea cave illuminated by an other-worldly blue light. The easiest way to visit is to take a boat **tour** (Map p112, E1; ☎081 837 56 46; www.motoscafisticapri.com; Private Pier 0; Grotta Azzurra/island trip €15/€18) from Marina Grande; tickets include the return boat trip but the rowing boat into the cave and admission are paid separately. Beautiful though it is, the Grotta is extremely popular in the summer and the crowds coupled with long waiting times and tip-hungry guides can make the experience underwhelming for some.

Measuring 54m by 30m and rising to a height of 15m, the grotto is said to have sunk by up to 20m in prehistoric times, blocking every opening except the 1.3m-high entrance. And this is the key to the magical blue light. Sunlight enters through a small underwater aperture and is refracted through the water; this, combined with the reflection of the light off the white sandy seafloor, produces the vivid blue effect to which the cave owes its name.

Bear in mind that the time actually spent in the Grotta during a tour amounts to 10 minutes maximum. The singing row-boat 'captains' are included in the price, so don't feel any obligation if they push for a tip.

Eating

Il Geranio SEAFOOD $$$

5 MAP P112, F6

Time to pop the question or quell those pre-departure blues? The terrace at this sophisticated spot offers heart-stealing views over the pine trees to Isole Faraglioni. Seafood is the speciality, particularly the salt-baked fish. Other fine choices include octopus salad and linguine with saffron and mussels. Book at least three days ahead for a terrace table in high season. (☎081 837 06 16; www.geraniocapri.com; Via Matteotti 8; meals €45-50; ⏲noon-3pm & 7-11pm mid-Apr–mid-Oct)

È Divino ITALIAN $$

6 MAP P112, F4

Proudly eccentric (what other restaurant has a bed in its dining room?), this diligent purveyor of Slow Food is a precious secret to those who know it. Whether dining among lemon trees in the garden or among antiques, chandeliers and contemporary art (and that bed!) inside, expect a thoughtful, regularly changing menu dictated by what's fresh from the garden and market. (☎081 837 83 64;

SELINA IRINA/SHUTTERSTOCK ©

Giardini di Augusto (p114)

www.edivinocapri.com/divino; Via Sella Orta 10a; meals €33-48; 8pm-1am daily Jun-Aug, 12.30-2.30pm & 7.30pm-midnight Tue-Sun rest of the year;)

Raffaele Buonacore

FAST FOOD $

7 MAP P112, F4

Ideal for a quick takeaway, this popular, down-to-earth snack bar does a roaring trade in savoury and sweet treats. Hit the spot with *panini* (sandwiches), stuffed peppers, waffles and the legendary ice cream. Hard to beat, though, are the delicate but filling *sfogliatelle* (cinnamon-infused ricotta in a puff-pastry shell; €2.50) and the feather-light speciality *caprilu al limone* (lemon and almond cakes). (081 837 78 26; Via Vittorio Emanuele III 35; snacks €2-10, gelato from €2.50; 8am-9pm, closed Tue Oct-Jun;)

Al Grottino

NEAPOLITAN $$

8 MAP P112, F4

Expect a queue here. Dating from 1937, Al Grottino was a VIP spot in the '50s and '60s (check out the photos in the window), and it continues to lure locals and visitors with traditional Neapolitan dishes like *ravioli alla caprese* (pasta filled with ricotta, parmigiano reggiano and marjoram) and specials like *cocotte* (handmade pasta with mixed seafood served in a paella-like pan). (081 837 05 84; www.ristorantealgrottino.net; Via Longano 27; meals from €30; 11.45am-3.30pm & 6.30pm-midnight Apr-Oct)

La Capannina
TRATTORIA $$$

9 MAP P112, F4

Dating back to 1931, this is the island's most famous traditional trattoria and a long-time favourite on the celebrity circuit. Set up to look like a Hollywood version of a rustic resturant it serves a classic island menu of comfort food. Reservations are recommended. (081 837 07 32; www.capannina capri.com; Via le Botteghe 12; meals €40-50; noon-3pm & 7-11.30pm mid-Mar–Oct)

Drinking

Taverna Anema e Core
CLUB

10 MAP P112, F4

Behind a humble exterior is one of the island's most famous nightspots, run by the charismatic Guido Lembo. This smooth and sophisticated bar-club attracts an appealing mix of super-chic and casually dressed punters, here for the relaxed atmosphere and regular live music, including unwaveringly authentic Neapolitan guitar strumming and singing. (329 4742508; www.anemaecore.com; Vico Sella Orta 39e; 11pm-late Tue-Sun)

Shopping

La Parissienne
FASHION & ACCESSORIES

11 MAP P112, F4

First opened in 1906 (yes, that is not a misprint!), and best known for introducing Capri pants in the 1960s – famously worn by Audrey Hepburn, who bought them here – La Parissienne can run you up a made-to-measure pair within a day. It also sells off-the-hook Capri pants (from €250). (081 837 02 83; www.laparisiennecapri.it; Piazza Umberto I 7; 9am-10pm)

Carthusia I Profumi di Capri
COSMETICS

12 MAP P112, F5

Allegedly, Capri's famous floral perfume was established in 1380 by the prior of the Certosa di San Giacomo. Caught unawares by a royal visit, he displayed the island's most beautiful flowers for the queen. Changing the water in the vase, he discovered a floral scent. This became the base of the classic perfume now sold at this smart laboratory outlet. (081 837 53 93; www.carthusia.it; Via Matteotti 2d; 9am-8pm Apr-Sep, to 5pm rest of year)

Da Costanzo
SHOES

13 MAP P112, E5

In 1959 Clarke Gable stopped off at this tiny, unpretentious shoe shop to get a pair of handmade leather sandals, and the shop still sells a range of colourful styles to passers-by and shoe aficionados. Prices start at around €90 – a small investment for a piece of Hollywood history. (081 837 80 77; Via Roma 49; 9am-8.30pm Mar-Nov)

Walking Tour

Procida Island Walk

Of the three main islands in the Gulf of Naples, Procida is the least visited and, by definition, the most down-to-earth. Lob a football along the main street and you're more likely to hit a local than a tourist, stumbling from bar to fishing skiff, or ambling along the Via Vittorio Emanuele on their way back from Sunday Mass.

Getting There

Procida is accessible by ferry and hydrofoil; both arrive at Marina Grande.

There are multiple connections to Naples with Caremar (40 minutes, eight daily) and SNAV (25 minutes).

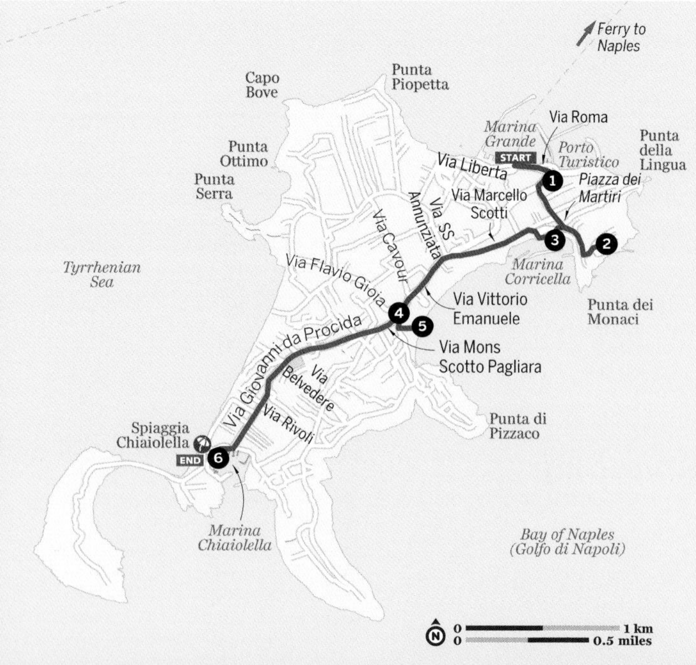

❶ Bar dal Cavaliere

Step off the hydrofoil straight into the portside **Cavaliere** (081 810 10 74; Via Roma 42, Marina Grande; pastries from €1; 7am-midnight) where you can get acquainted with Procida's one essential delicacy, the *lingua di bue* – a flaky pastry with a creamy lemon filling. Sink a scalding espresso on the side and be on your merry way.

❷ Terra Murata

Life here has never strayed too far from Procida's fortified **Terra Murata** (walled town) positioned like an eyrie on the highest part of the island and covered in a coil of narrow, twisting streets that haven't changed much since medieval times. Here you'll find an abbey, a sentinel church, an old palace turned prison, and the ghosts of Procidians past.

❸ Marina Corricella

Procida's handsomely weathered harbour is more old fishing village than modern marina, with wooden boats sitting alongside piles of nets and sea breezes fanning lines of drying washing. Populated by tall, warped houses painted in a broad palate of pastel colours, it's a cheerful place full of decent bars and seafood restaurants, and completely free of traffic (cars can't enter).

❹ Piazza Olmo

The centre of the island and the centre of everyday life on sleepy Procida, this diminutive road junction is a good place to take pot luck and wander down a narrow lane to see where it takes you (to the sea within 15 minutes). Dented vespas lean against paint-peeled buildings and elderly residents gossip in shop doorways.

❺ Spiaggia di Chiaia

With its weather-beaten jetty, ocean-embracing seafood restaurant and views of Marina Corricella piled on a cliff in the distance, this long narrow beach has a loyal local following. Enter via a 'secret' stairway (or sail in), order a pile of grilled and fried fish in **La Conchiglia** (081 896 76 02; www.laconchigliaristorante.com; Via Pizzaco 10, Solchiaro; meals €25; 1-3.30pm & 8-9.30pm summer), and let the waves lull you into an afternoon siesta.

❻ Marina Chiaiolella

Procida's 'third' marina is the furthest from the port and is thus less frequented by visitors. Set in a sheltered bay (an extinct volcanic crater), it preserves the air of a self-contained fishing village with its church, main street and array of good restaurants. Stroll through the Santa Margherita neighbourhood to the south for a view of the **Isola di Vivara** (347 7858256; www.comune.procida.na.it; adult/reduced €10/5; guided tours 10am & 3pm Fri-Sun) nature reserve.

Explore

Sorrento & the Amalfi Coast

The Amalfi Coast is one of Italy's most bewitching destinations. Mountains plunge into the sea in a nail-biting vertical scene of crags, cliff-clinging abodes and verdant woodland. From precipitous Positano to lofty Ravello, its string of fabled towns read like a Hollywood cast list. Its western gateway is Sorrento, a handsome clifftop resort that, despite the package tourism, retains its seductive southern soul.

Sorrento's bustling heart is Piazza Tasso, with many of the town's sights in the streets of the centro storico *(p134) directly to the west of it. These include the Basilica di Sant'Antonino (p136) and the Museo Bottega della Tarsia Lignea (p135). The town's best bathing spot, Bagni Regina Giovanna (p135), is also to the west, though further out of town. East of Sorrento, both the Amalfi Coast jewels of Positano (p122) and Ravello (p128) can be tackled as day trips, though it's worth spending a night in each to slow down the pace and properly soak up their charms.*

Getting There & Around

Circumvesuviana trains run to Naples via Pompeii and Ercolano.

SITA Sud buses serve Naples and the Amalfi Coast, leaving from the bus station across from the Circumvesuviana train station.

Sorrento is the main jumping-off point for Capri and also has ferry connections to Naples and Amalfi coastal resorts during the summer months.

Sorrento Map on p132

View of Amalfi Coast from Ravello (p128) JAVEN/SHUTTERSTOCK ©

Top Experience

Behold Positano

Deluxe, dramatic Positano is the Amalfi Coast's pin-up, its vertiginous houses tumbling down to the sea in a cascade of sun-bleached peach, pink and terracotta. Its steep streets and steps are no less photogenic, flanked by wisteria-draped hotels, smart restaurants and fashionable boutiques. Yet, despite its celebrity status, a southern-Italian holiday feel lingers, from its crumbling stucco to its pizza-chowing sunbathers.

Tourist Office

089 87 50 67

www.aziendaturismo positano.it

Via Regina Giovanna 13

8.30am-8pm Mon-Sat, to 2pm Sun May-Sep, reduced hours rest of year

Cultural Sights

Omnipresent in most Positano photos is the colourful majolica-tiled dome of its main church, the **Chiesa di Santa Maria Assunta** (089 87 54 80; Piazza Flavio Gioia; 8am-noon & 4-9pm). The church is known for a 13th-century Byzantine *Black Madonna and Child* above the main altar. The icon was supposedly stolen from Constantinople by pirates and smuggled west. A handsome 18th-century bell tower stands separate from the main church building in the piazza out front. During restoration works on the square and the crypt, a Roman villa was discovered. If you are visiting at a weekend you will probably have the added perk of seeing a wedding; it's one of the most popular churches in southern Italy for exchanging vows.

Just west of the church, the **Palazzo Murat** (089 875 51 77; www.palazzomurat.it; Via dei Mulini 23) is now a luxury hotel. It may be beyond your budget to stay, but you can still visit the balmy flower-filled courtyard, have a drink on the vine-draped patio and contemplate the short, tragic life of flamboyant Joachim Murat, the 18th-century French king of Naples who had the palace built as a summer residence for himself and his wife, Caroline Bonaparte.

Nestled between trendy boutiques and lemon-themed ceramics shops, **Franco Senesi** (089 87 52 57; www.francosenesifineart.com; Via dei Mulini 16; 10am-midnight Apr-Nov) is a bold, uncluttered exhibition space with rooms showcasing work by over 20 Italian modern artists and sculptors. You can walk around without being hassled, admiring (and even buying) artworks varied enough to suit most tastes, spanning exquisite life drawings, colourful surrealistic landscapes and edgy abstract sculptures. Shipping can be arranged.

★ Top Tips

- April to June and October are less crowded periods, with June usually offering proper summer heat. The majority of hotels, restaurants and bars close from late October to Easter.
- Mobility Amalfi Coast runs local buses following the lower ring road every half-hour between 8am and midnight. Buy your ticket at tobacconists (€1.30) or on board.

Take a Break

- Positano has no shortage of commendable eateries, including lauded restaurants Casa Mele (p126) and, just out of town, Donna Rosa (p127).
- After dark, **Music on the Rocks** (089 87 58 74; www.musicontherocks.it; Via Grotte dell'Incanto 51; cover charge €10-30; 10pm-late Apr-Oct;) spins mainstream house and retro disco at what is one the best nightclubs on the Amalfi Coast.

Beaches & Boating

Positano's **Spiaggia Grande** probably isn't anyone's idea of a dream beach, with greyish sand covered by legions of bright umbrellas lined up like parked cars – and expensive cars at that. Hiring a chair and umbrella in the fenced-off areas costs around €20 per person per day (plus extra for showers). Fortunately, the crowded public areas are free and the toilets are spotlessly clean – as is the seawater.

From Spiaggia Grande, it's a gentle walk west, with an acceptable number of steps (hooray!) to **Spiaggia del Fornillo**. Toss off your stilettos and lace up your trainers: Fornillo is more laid-back than its swanky neighbour and it's also home to a handful of summer beach bars, which can get quite spirited after sunset. To reach it, head for the western end of Spiaggia Grande, by the ferry harbour, and climb the steps. Walk past the Torre Trasita and continue on as the path passes dramatic rock formations and a verdant gully until you reach the appealing beach.

Operating out of a kiosk near Positano's ferry terminal, **L'Uomo e il Mare** (089 81 16 13; www.escursioniluomoeilmare.it; 9am-8pm Easter-Oct) offers a range of tours, including Capri and Amalfi day trips (from €65 to €80). The outfit also organises private sunset tours to Li Galli, complete with champagne (from €200 for up to 12 people). Private tours should be organised at least a day in advance.

Retail Therapy

Positano's labyrinthine streets harbour a plethora of boutiques, peddling everything from handcrafted ceramics to chichi beachwear and sandals. **La Bottega di Brunella** (089 87 52 28; www.brunella.it; Viale Pasitea 72; 9am-9pm) is one of the reasons local women always look so effortlessly chic. It's one of just a handful of boutiques where the clothes are designed and made in Positano (most boutiques import despite the sometimes deceptive labelling). The garments here are made from pure linen and silk, the colours are earthy shades of cream, ochre, brown and yellow. There are two other branches in town, including a smaller boutique opposite Palazzo Murat.

For sumptuous, locally produced ceramics, hit **Ceramiche Maria Grazia** (089 812 34 81; Viale Pasitea 8; 9.30am-8.30pm May-Oct). The colours and designs are subtle and sophisticated, with lots of lemons emblazoned onto urns, plates, tables and even egg cups. To avoid stress at check-in time, consider going for the shipping option.

If your feet need a makeover, **La Botteguccia de Giovanni** (089 81 18 24; www.labottegucciapositano.it; Via Regina Giovanni 19; 9.30am-9pm May-Oct) is where craftsman Giovanni creates handmade leather sandals in his small workroom at the back of the shop. Choose a colour and any decorative flourishes you want (shells are somehow particularly well-suited to Positano...), tell him your size and then nip round

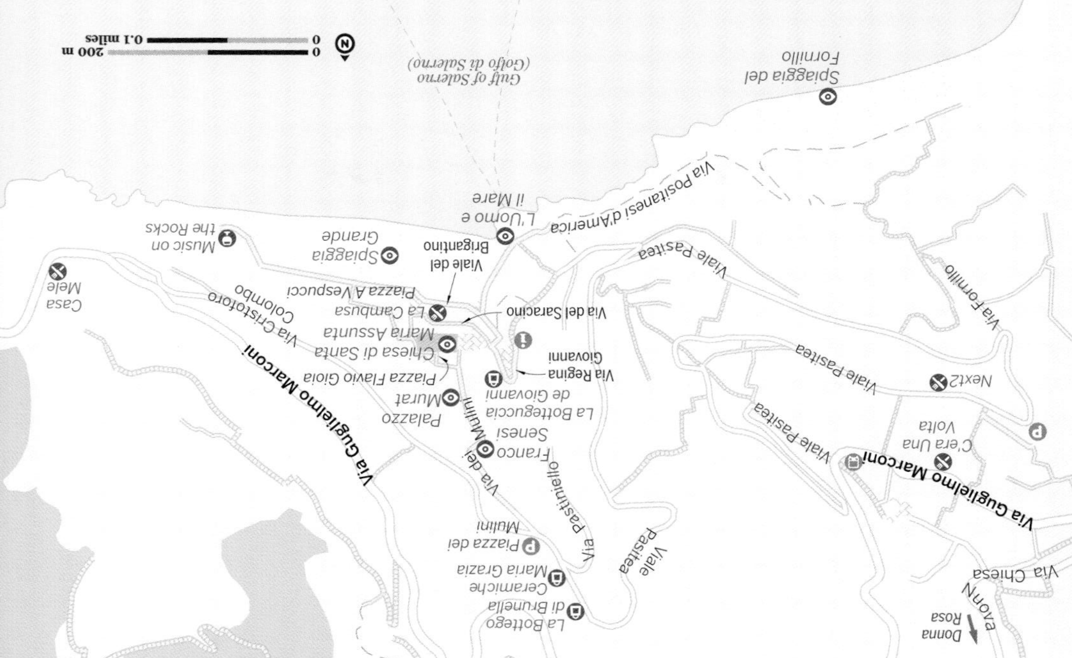

Via Guglielmo Marconi
Casa Mele
Music on the Rocks
Via Cristoforo Colombo
Piazza Flavio Gioia
Chiesa di Santa Maria Assunta
La Cambusa
Piazza A Vespucci
Spiaggia Grande
Palazzo Murat
Viale del Brigantino
Via dei Mulini
Franco Senesi
La Botteguccia de Giovanni
Via Regina Giovanni
Via del Saracino
L'Uomo e il Mare
La Bottego di Brunella
Ceramiche Maria Grazia
Piazza dei Mulini
Via Pastiniello
Viale Pasitea
Via Positanesi d'America
Gulf of Salerno
(Golfo di Salerno)
Spiaggia del Fornillo
Via Guglielmo Marconi
C'era Una Volta
Next2
Via Fornillo
Via Chiesa
Nuova
Donna Rosa
0 200 m
0 0.1 miles

the corner for a cappuccino while he makes your shoes. Prices start at around €50.

Food-Lover Standouts

Positano's pleasures extend to the palate. Indeed, some of the Amalfi Coast's best restaurants call Positano and its surrounds home. **Casa Mele** (089 81 13 64; www.casamele.com; Via Marconi 76; tasting menu €65-80; 7pm-midnight Tue-Sun Apr-early Dec) is one of those cool, contemporary restaurants with a lengthy tasting menu and food presented as art – and theatre. The open kitchen is a high-powered food laboratory from which emerge whimsical pastas, delicate fish in subtle sauces, and outstanding desserts. Service is equally sublime. It also runs three-hour cooking courses; check the website for details.

Further west in the town, equally contemporary **Next2** (089 812 35 16; www.next2.it; Viale Pasitea 242; meals from €50; 6.30-11pm Apr-Oct) offers subtle culinary twists. Here, local and organic ingredients are put to impressive use in dishes such as grilled octopus with baked olives and crunchy biscuit bread, or lamb ravioli with leek and deep-fried artichokes.

If you prefer your seafood by the beach, **La Cambusa** (089 87 54 32; www.lacambusapositano.com; Piazza Vespucci 4; meals €40; noon-11pm mid-Dec–Oct;) comes with a seafront terrace. Given the number of cash-rich tourists in these parts, this could easily equal high prices for less-than-average food.

Positano streetscape below Chiesa di Santa Maria Assunta (p123)

ROMAN BABAKIN/SHUTTERSTOCK ©

A Positano Hike

Positano's hilly hinterland harbours some satisfying walks, among them the 9km **Santa Maria del Castello Circuit**. The advantage of this particular circuitous route is that it enjoys a bit of shade in its early stages as you plod heavenward amid a thick and gnarly holm-oak forest.

The walk starts on the main coast road (SS163) close to the Montepertuso turn-off by a ruined building and climbs steeply through trees before breaking into dryer Mediterranean scrub higher up. The coastal views open out as the path (#333a) traverses the hills above Positano with the hulk of Monte Sant'Angelo standing sentinel in the background. Turn left 2km up the ascent and then right at the top to join a wider trail towards the hike's high point, the tiny village of Santa Maria del Castello (670m) accessible by diverting along a narrow, paved road. At this ancient crossing point around 5km into the hike, you'll find a small bar and a church. Take the narrow road back down to the main path; turn left (trail #333), proceed around the headland and then head right on a path that leads steeply down via a series of well-constructed staircases to Positano, visible in all its glory directly below. The walk ends beside the **Bar Internazionale** (Via Guglielmo Marconi 306; ⌚7am-1am) in Upper Positano.

Thankfully, that is not the case, la Cambusa's top-notch ingredients shining brightly in dishes such as homemade crab-filled ravioli and seafood risotto.

One of the area's most celebrated restaurants lies just above Positano, in the hilltop village of Montepertuso. Indeed, despite its out-of-the-way location, **Donna Rosa** (☎089 81 18 06; www.drpositano.com; Via Montepertuso 97-99; meals €45-65; ⌚11am-2pm & 5.30-9.30pm Wed-Mon Apr-Dec, closed lunch Aug) is never short of fawning food lovers. The reason: outstanding food served by three generations of the original Rosa's family and a nod of admiration from that well-known food-campaigning Italophile, Jamie Oliver. Reservations are highly recommended for dinner and obligatory at lunch.

While many of Positano's restaurants are at the higher end of the price scale, cheaper standouts do exist. Among them is **C'era Una Volta** (☎089 81 19 30; Via Marconi 127; meals €20-30; ⌚noon-3pm & 6.30-11pm), a heroically authentic trattoria at the top of town. The menu here is all about honest, down-to-earth regional grub, including a commendable *gnocchi alla sorrentina* (gnocchi in a tomato and basil sauce). It also serves pizzas (from €4.50), cheap beer and runs a free shuttle to/from the town centre in the summer.

Top Experience

Climb in Ravello

It cured Richard Wagner's writer's block and impressed American writer Gore Vidal so much that he stayed for 30 years. Ravello has a metamorphic effect on people. Founded in the 5th century as a sanctuary from barbarian invaders fresh from sacking Rome, the Amalfi Coast's most famous hilltop town is second only to Positano in the style and glamour stakes.

Tourist Office

☎ 089 85 70 96

www.ravellotime.it

Piazza Fontana Moresca 10

🕒 10am-8pm

Villas & Fabled Gardens

Villa Rufolo

To the south of Ravello's cathedral (Duomo), a 14th-century tower marks the entrance to **Villa Rufolo** (☎089 85 76 21; www.villarufolo.it; Piazza Duomo; adult/reduced €7/5; ⏰9am-9pm May-Sep, reduced hours Oct-Apr, tower museum 11am-4pm), famed for its beautiful cascading gardens. Created by a Scotsman, Francis Neville Reid, in 1853, they are truly magnificent, commanding divine panoramic views packed with exotic colours, artistically crumbling towers and luxurious blooms. Note that the gardens are at their best from May till October; they don't merit the entrance fee outside those times.

The villa was built in the 13th century for the wealthy Rufolo dynasty and was home to several popes as well as king Robert of Anjou. Wagner was so inspired by the gardens when he visited in 1880 that he modelled the garden of Klingsor (the setting for the second act of the opera Parsifal) on them.

The 13th-century Torre Maggiore (Main Tower) now houses the **Torre-Museo**, an interactive museum that sheds light on the villa's history and characters. Among the latter is Sir Francis Neville Reid, the Scottish botanist who purchased and extensively restored the property in the 19th century. The museum also showcases art, archaeological finds and ceramics linked to the villa. Stairs inside the tower lead up to an outdoor viewing platform, affording knockout views of the villa and the Amalfi Coast.

Today Villa Rufolo's gardens stage world-class concerts during the town's classical music **festival** (☎089 85 84 22; www.ravellofestival.com; ⏰Jul-Sep). Indeed, between early July and September, the Ravello Festival turns much of the town centre into a stage, with events ranging from orchestral concerts and chamber music to ballet performances, film screenings and exhibitions.

★ Top Tips

- Book accommodation well ahead for summer – especially during the annual Ravello Festival.
- Hone your culinary skills with a cooking course at **Mamma Agata** (☎089 85 70 19; www.mammaagata.com; Piazza San Cosma 9; courses €250). A one-day demonstration class culminates in sipping and supping on a sea-view terrace.

✕ Take a Break

- With spectacular terrace views, **Da Salvatore** (☎089 85 72 27; www.salvatoreravello.com; Via della Republicca 2; meals €38-45; ⏰12.30-3pm & 7.30-10pm Tue-Sun Easter-Nov) creates dishes with flair and flavour. Wood-fired pizzas are available in the evenings.
- Deli-cafe **Babel** (☎089 858 62 15; Via Trinità 13; meals €20; ⏰11.30am-3.30pm & 7-11pm Thu-Tue mid-Jun–mid-Sep, closed Jan & Feb; 📶) offers affordable Italian tapas-style dishes, creative salads and excellent local wines.

Villa Cimbrone

If you could bottle up a take-away image of the Amalfi, it might be the view from the Belvedere of Infinity, classical busts in the foreground, craggy coast splashed with pastel-shaded villages in the background. It's yours to admire at the refashioned 11th-century **Villa Cimbrone** (☎089 85 74 59; www.hotelvillacimbrone.com/gardens; Via Santa Chiara 26; adult/reduced €7/4; ⏰9am-sunset), now an upmarket hotel with sublime gardens. Open to the public, the gardens were mainly created by a British peer, Ernest Beckett, who reconfigured them with rose beds, temples and a Moorish pavilion in the early 1900s. The villa (also owned by Beckett) was something of a bohemian retreat in its early days; it was frequented by Greta Garbo and her lover Leopold Stokowski as a secret hideaway. Other illustrious former guests include Virginia Woolf, Winston Churchill, DH Lawrence and Salvador Dalí. The house and gardens sit atop a crag a 10-minute walk south of Piazza Duomo.

Piazza Duomo

Ravello's refinement is exemplified in the town's polished main piazza where debonair diners relax under the canopies of alfresco cafes. Forming the piazza's eastern flank is the **Duomo** (www.chiesaravello.com; Piazza Duomo; museum adult/reduced €3/1.50; ⏰8am-9pm), built in 1086 and guilty of various nips and tucks over the centuries. The facade is 16th century, but the central bronze door, one of only about two dozen in the country, dates from 1179. The interior is a late 20th-century

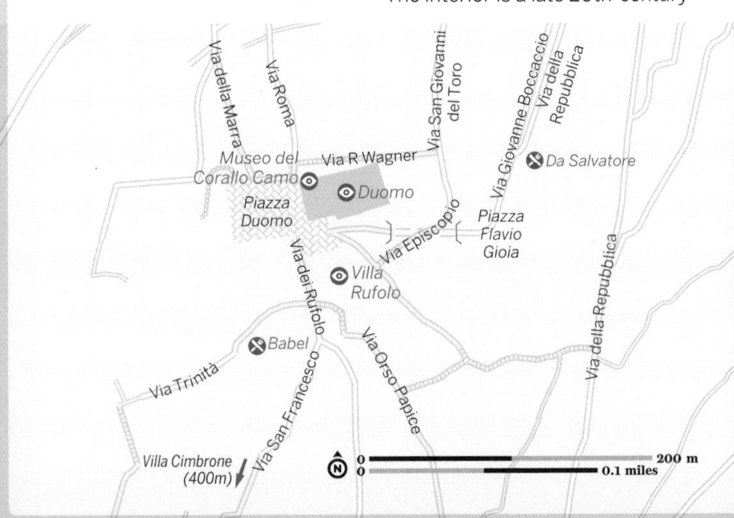

Ravello Rambles

Ravello is the starting point for numerous walks – some of which follow ancient paths through the surrounding Lattari mountains. If you've got the legs for it, you can walk down to **Minori** via an attractive route of steps, hidden alleys and olive groves, passing the picturesque hamlet of Torello en route. This 2.5km walk kicks off just to the left of Villa Rufolo and takes around 45 minutes. Alternatively, you can head the other way, to Amalfi, via the ancient village of **Scala**. Once a flourishing religious centre with more than a hundred churches, and the oldest settlement on the Amalfi Coast, Scala (2km from Ravello) is now a pocket-sized, sleepy place where the wind whistles through empty streets. In the central square, the Romanesque **duomo** (Piazza Municipio; ⏲8am-noon & 5-7pm) retains some of its 12th-century solemnity. Ask at the Ravello tourist office for more information on local walks.

interpretation of what the original must have once looked like.

Drawing it above the rank of a run-of-the-mill church is the striking pulpit, supported by six twisting columns set on marble lions and decorated with flamboyant mosaics of peacocks and other birds. Note also how the floor is tilted towards the square – a deliberate measure to enhance the perspective effect. The cathedral museum claims a modest collection of religious artefacts.

The piazza is also home to the **Museo del Corallo Camo** (☎089 85 74 61; www.museodelcorallo.com; Piazza Duomo 9; ⏲10am-noon & 3-5pm Mon-Sat). Ostensibly a cameo shop selling engraved gems with raised reliefs crafted primarily out of coral and shell, it also harbours a small museum beyond the showroom. The museum's magnificent pieces include a mid-16th-century Madonna, a 3rd-century-AD Roman amphora, gorgeous tortoiseshell combs and some exquisite oil paintings. Refreshingly, Camo is the antithesis of the overpriced shops in the centre of Ravello and owner Giorgio's cameos have been commissioned by all kinds of well-known identities, including Hillary Clinton and actress Susan Sarandon. That said, you may think twice about the ethics of buying coral.

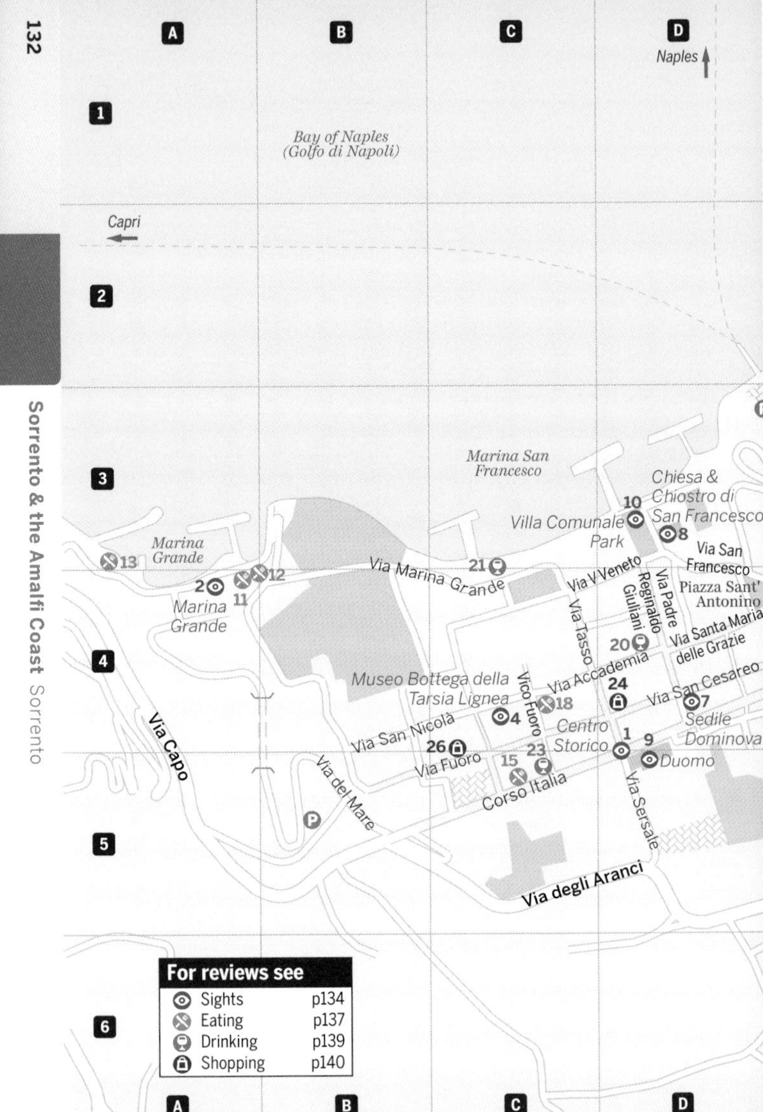
A
B
C
D
Naples
1
Bay of Naples (Golfo di Napoli)
Capri
2
3
Marina San Francesco
Chiesa & Chiostro di San Francesco
10
Villa Comunale Park
8
Via San Francesco
Marina Grande
13
2
11
12
Marina Grande
Via Marina Grande
21
Via V Veneto
Piazza Sant' Antonino
Via Padre Reginaldo Giuliani
Via Tasso
Via Santa Maria delle Grazie
20
4
Via Accademia
Museo Bottega della Tarsia Lignea
Vico Fuoro
24
Via San Cesareo
7
18
4
Sedile Dominova
Via Capo
Via San Nicolà
Centro Storico
1
9
26
23
Duomo
Via Fuoro
15
Via del Mare
Corso Italia
Via Sersale
P
5
Via degli Aranci
For reviews see
Sights p134
Eating p137
Drinking p139
Shopping p140
6
A
B
C
D

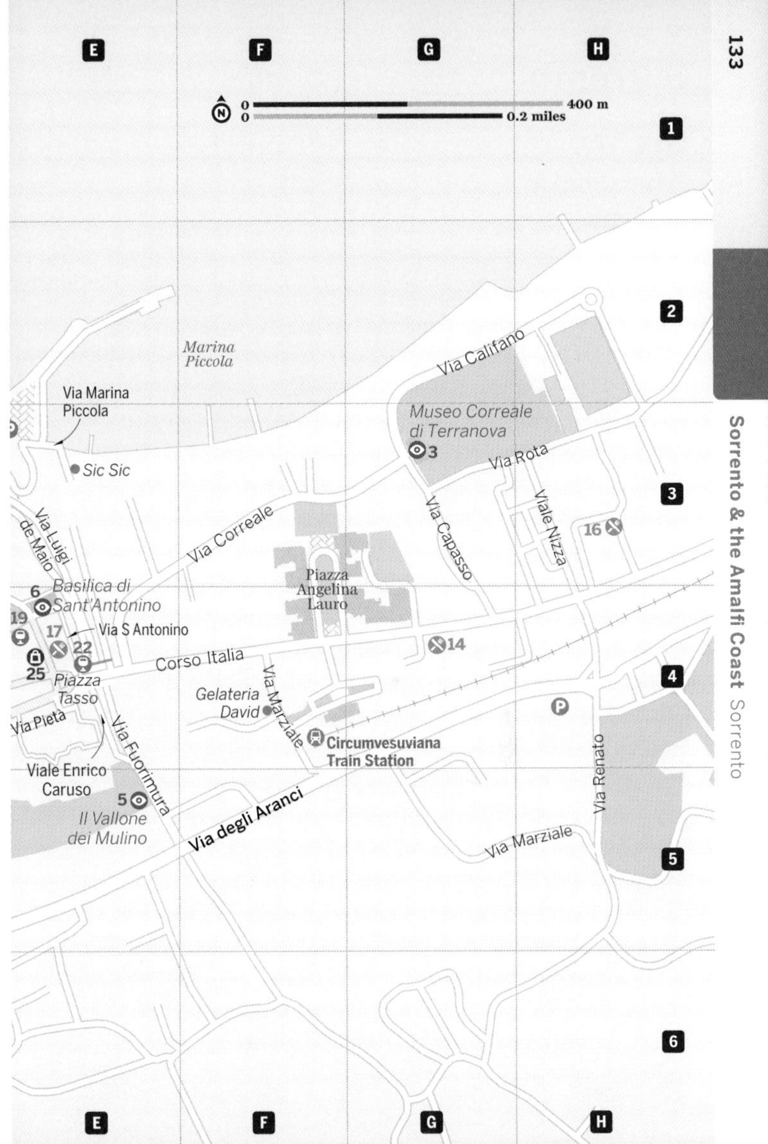

E
F
G
H
0
400 m
0
0.2 miles
1
2
3
4
5
6
Marina Piccola
Via Marina Piccola
Sic Sic
Via Califano
Museo Correale di Terranova
3
Via Rota
Via Luigi de Maio
Via Correale
Via Capasso
Viale Nizza
16
Piazza Angelina Lauro
6
Basilica di Sant'Antonino
19
17
Via S Antonino
22
25
Corso Italia
14
Piazza Tasso
Via Pietà
Via Marziale
Gelateria David
Circumvesuviana Train Station
Viale Enrico Caruso
Via Fuorimura
5
Il Vallone dei Mulino
Via degli Aranci
Via Renato
Via Marziale

Sorrento

Sights

Centro Storico

AREA

1 MAP P132, D5

A major hub for shops, restaurants and bars, recently pedestrianised Corso Italia is the main thoroughfare shooting east–west through the bustling *centro storico* (historic centre). Duck into the side streets to the north and you'll find narrow lanes flanked by traditional green-shuttered buildings, interspersed with the occasional *palazzo* (mansion), piazza or church. Souvenir and antiques shops, fashion boutiques, trattorias and some fine old buildings also jostle for space in this grid of cobbled backstreets.

Marina Grande

HARBOUR

2 MAP P132, A4

Noticeably detached from the main city and bereft of the hydrofoils and ferries that crowd Marina Piccola, this secluded former fishing village has a timeless maritime air not dissimilar to Marina Corricella on Procida. Bobbing fishing boats and pastel-coloured houses add character to a quarter that's known for its family-run seafood restaurants. The marina also protects the closest thing in Sorrento to a *spiaggia* (beach). (Via Marina Grande)

Marina Grande

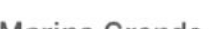

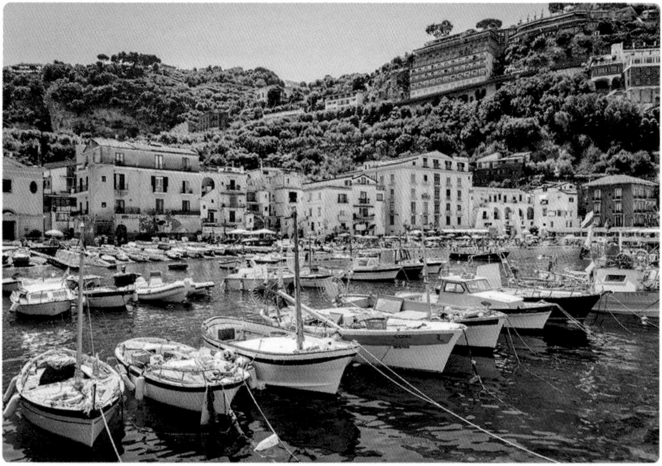

ALEXANDER LUKATSKIY/SHUTTERSTOCK ©

Museo Correale di Terranova

MUSEUM

3 MAP P132, G3

East of the city centre, this wide-ranging museum is well worth a visit whether you're a clock collector, an archaeological egghead or into delicate ceramics. In addition to the rich assortment of 16th- to 19th-century Neapolitan art and crafts (including extraordinary examples of marquetry), you'll discover Japanese, Chinese and European ceramics, clocks, fans and, on the ground floor, ancient and medieval artefacts. Among these is a fragment of an ancient Egyptian carving uncovered in the vicinity of Sorrento's Sedile Dominova (p136). (081 878 18 46; www.museocorreale.it; Via Correale 50; adult/reduced €8/3; 9.30am-6.30pm Mon-Fri, to 1.30pm Sat Apr-Oct, 9.30am-1.30pm Tue-Sun Nov-Mar)

Museo Bottega della Tarsia Lignea

MUSEUM

4 MAP P132, C4

Since the 18th century, Sorrento has been famous for its *intarsio* (marquetry) furniture, made with elaborately designed inlaid wood. Some wonderful historical examples can be found in this museum, many of them etched in the once fashionable picaresque style. The museum, housed in an 18th-century palace complete with beautiful frescoes, also has an interesting collection of paintings, prints and photographs depicting the town and the surrounding area in the 19th century. (081 877 19 42; Via San Nicola 28; adult/reduced €8/5; 10am-6.30pm Apr-Oct, to 5pm Nov-Mar)

Coastal Pleasures

Sorrento lacks a decent beach, so consider heading to **Bagni Regina Giovanna**, a rocky option with clear, clean water about 2km west of town. It's possible to walk here (follow Via Capo), but wear good shoes as it's a bit of a scramble.

Alternatively, seek out the best beaches by renting a boat from **Sic Sic** (Map p132, E3; 081 807 22 83; www.nauticasicsic.com; May-Oct) in Marina Piccola. Boats can be rented with or without a skipper, with a variety of motor boats starting at around €50 per hour or from €150 per day plus fuel. It also organises boat excursions.

Il Vallone dei Mulino

HISTORIC SITE

5 MAP P132, E5

Just behind Piazza Tasso, a vertiginous natural phenomenon is on view from Via Fuorimura. Il Vallone dei Mulino is a deep mountain cleft that dates from a volcanic eruption 35,000 years ago. Sorrento was once bounded by three gorges, but today this is the only one that remains. The valley is named after the ancient wheat mills that were once located here. The weed-covered ruins of one are still clearly visible. (Valley of the Mills; Via Fuorimura)

Basilica di Sant'Antonino CHURCH

6 MAP P132, E4

Named after Sorrento's patron saint, the town's oldest church barely looks like a church at all from the outside. The interior paints a more ecclesial picture with its Roman artefacts, dark medieval paintings, gilded ceiling, and the oddity of two whale ribs in the lobby by the front door. Apparently, the much-loved saint performed numerous miracles, including one in which he rescued a child from a whale's stomach. The saint's bones lie beneath the baroque interior in an 18th-century crypt. (081 878 14 37; Piazza Sant' Antonino; 9am-noon & 5-7pm)

Sedile Dominova HISTORIC BUILDING

7 MAP P132, D4

Incongruously wedged between racks of lemon-themed souvenir merchandise, this 15th-century domed *palazzo* has exquisite, albeit faded, original frescoes. Crowned by a cupola, the terrace, open to the street on two sides, was originally a meeting point for the town's medieval aristocracy; today it houses a working-men's club where local pensioners sit around playing cards. (Via San Cesareo)

Chiesa & Chiostro di San Francesco CHURCH

8 MAP P132, D3

Located next to the Villa Comunale Park, this church is best known for the peaceful 14th-century cloister abutting it, which is accessible via a small door from the church. The courtyard features an Arabic portico and interlaced arches supported by octagonal pillars. Replete with bougainvillea and birdsong, they're built on the ruins of a 7th-century monastery. Upstairs in the Sorrento International Photo School, the **Gallery Celentano** (344 083 85 03; www.raffaelecelentano.com; adult/reduced €2.50/free; 10am-8pm Mar-Dec) exhibits black-and-white photographs of Italian life and landscapes by contemporary local photographer Raffaele Celentano. (Via San Francesco; 8am-1pm & 2-8pm)

Duomo CATHEDRAL

9 MAP P132, D5

Sorrento's cathedral features a striking exterior fresco, a triple-tiered bell tower, four classical columns and an elegant majolica clock. Inside, take note of the marble bishop's throne (1573), as well as both the wooden choir stalls and stations of the cross, decorated in the local *intarsio* (marquetry) style. Although the cathedral's original structure dates from the 15th century, the building has been altered several times, most recently in the early 20th century when the current facade was added. (☎081 878 22 48; Corso Italia; ⏰8am-12.30pm & 4.30-9pm)

Villa Comunale Park PARK

10 MAP P132, D3

This lofty park is more about vistas than greenery, perched atop Sorrento's famous cliffs with commanding views across the bay to Mt Vesuvius. With its operatic buskers and small **bar** (☎081 807 40 90; www.lavillasorrento.it; Villa Comunale; ⏰8.30am-11pm; 📶), it's particularly popular at sunset. A lift (€1) at its western edge leads down to the port. (admission free; ⏰8am-1am Jun-Aug, to midnight May & Sep, reduced hours rest of year)

Eating

O'Puledrone SEAFOOD €€

11 MAP P132, A4

The best fish you eat in Sorrento might be one you caught, a viable proposition at this congenial joint on the harbour at Marina Grande run by a cooperative of local fishers. Let them take you out on a three-hour fishing trip (€70) and the chef will cook your catch and serve it to you with a carafe of wine. (☎081 012 41 34; www.opuledrone.com; Via Marina Grande 150; meals €25-30; ⏰noon-3pm & 6.30pm-late Apr-Oct)

Cooking Up a Storm

Culinary types can opt for a serious culinary vacation or one of the popular four-hour classes (€75) at **Sorrento Cooking School** (☎081 878 35 55; www.sorrentocookingschool.com; Viale dei Pini 52, Sant'Agnello; ⏰10am-2pm Apr-Oct), where you can learn to make pizza, ravioli and tiramisu in a beautiful spot surrounded by lemon trees.

If you're a sweet tooth, **Gelateria David** (Map p132, F4; ☎081 807 36 49; www.gelateriadavidsorrento.it; Via Marziale 19; ⏰8am-1am) runs gelato-making classes (€12), which last around an hour. Times vary according to demand, so call or drop by to organise.

Da Emilia TRATTORIA €€

12 MAP P132, A4

Founded in 1947 and still run by the same family, this is a friendly, fast-moving joint overlooking the fishing boats in Marina Grande. There's a large informal dining room, complete with youthful photos of former patron Sophia Loren, a romantic terrace by lapping waves, and a menu of straightforward dishes such as mussels with lemon, clam spaghetti and grilled calamari. (☎081 807 27 20; www.daemilia.it; Via Marina Grande 62; meals €22-30; ⏰noon-3pm & 6-10.30pm Mar-Nov; 👪)

Soul & Fish

SEAFOOD €€

13 MAP P132, A3

Soul & Fish has a hipper vibe than Marina Grande's no-nonsense seafood restaurants. Your bread comes in a bag, your dessert in a Kilner jar and your freshly grilled fish with a waiter ready to slice it up before your eyes. The decor is more chic beach shack than sea-shanty dive bar, with wooden decks, director chairs and puffy cushions. (081 878 21 70; Marina Grande; meals €38-46; noon-2.30pm & 7-10.30pm, closed Nov-Easter;)

Pizzeria Da Franco

PIZZA €

14 MAP P132, G4

Casual Da Franco's long wooden tables are rarely short of customers, many of them here for the superlative pizza. Served in tin trays, it's made the Sorrento way, which means a crisper base than its Neapolitan counterpart. Those hulking Parma *prosciutti* suspended above you also appear on the list of *antipasti*, which include traditional local salami, cheeses and grilled veggies. (081 877 20 66; Corso Italia 265; pizzas from €6; 9am-2am;)

AZZ!

TAVERNA €

15 MAP P132, C5

Like an Italian 'caff' without the greasy spoons, AZZ! delights in its simplicity. Pungent garlic bread, intense lasagna and an appetite-quenching *spaghetti puttanesca* are served at a speed best described as 'allegro' amid multilingual banter between customers and staff. Ideal if you're on your own, in a hurry, and don't want to be surrounded by romantic diners. (081 877 46 01; Corso Italia 14; mains & snacks €8-10; 9.30am-midnight)

La Cantinaccia del Popolo

NEAPOLITAN €

16 MAP P132, H3

Festooned with garlic and with cured hams hanging from the ceiling, this down-to-earth favourite proves that top-notch produce and simplicity are the keys to culinary success. A case in point is the *spaghetti al pomodoro*, a basic dish of pasta and tomato that bursts with flavour, vibrancy and balance. For extra authenticity, it's served directly to you in the pan. (366 1015497; Vico Terzo Rota 3; meals €21; 11am-3pm & 7-11pm Tue-Sun)

Zi'Ntonio

ITALIAN €€€

17 MAP P132, E4

Warm, buzzing and elegantly rustic, multilevel Zi'Ntonio draws everyone from local families and couples to clued-up out-of-towners. While earthy standouts include fried zucchini flowers stuffed with buffalo mozzarella and basil, as well as a soul-coaxing lentil and escarole *zuppa* (soup), keep your belly empty if opting for the cult-status *risotto alla pescatore*, a huge, flavour-packed paella-style dish laden with seafood. (081 878 16 23; www.zintonio.it; Via Luigi

De Maio 9-11; pizzas from €6, meals around €40; ⌚noon-3.30pm & 6pm-midnight)

Inn Bufalito

ITALIAN **€€**

18 MAP P132, C4

Owner Franco Coppola (no relation to the movie man) exudes a genuine passion for showcasing local produce in his rustic-chic mozzarella bar and restaurant. Buffalo mozzarella can be ordered as part of a tasting platter, while the buffalo itself makes an appearance in numerous dishes, from homemade *paccheri* (short, fat pasta tubes) with buffalo meat *ragù* to grilled buffalo steak. (☎081 365 69 75; www.innbufalito.it; Vico Fuoro 21; meals €25-30; ⌚noon-midnight; 📶 🥕)

Drinking

D'Anton

LOUNGE

19 MAP P132, E4

Welcome to a new and very Italian concept: a cocktail bar doubling up as an interior-design store. That elegant sofa you're sipping a negroni on is for sale. So is that glistening chandelier and that enchanting mirror. Add them to your drinks bill if you're feeling flush, or just admire the candelabras and lampshades over savoury *antipasti* and wicked chocolate-and-almond cake. (☎333 8075839; www.dantonsorrento.com; Piazza Sant'Antonio 3/4; ⌚5-10pm Mon, 10am-2pm & 5-10pm Tue-Thu, 10am-2pm & 5pm-midnight Fri-Sun)

Pizza margherita

Bollicine

WINE BAR

20 MAP P132, D4

The wine list at this unpretentious bar with a dark, woody interior includes all the big Italian names and a selection of interesting local labels. If you can't decide what to go for, the amiable bar staff will advise you. There's also a small menu of *panini* (sandwiches), bruschettas and one or two pasta dishes. (081 878 46 16; Via Accademia 9; 6.30pm-late)

La Pergola

BAR

21 MAP P132, C3

When love is in the air, put on your best Italian shoes and head for a pre-dinner libation at the Hotel Bellevue Syrene's swoon-inducing terrace bar-restaurant. With its commanding clifftop view across the Bay of Naples towards Mt Vesuvius, it never fails to glam up an otherwise ordinary evening. (081 878 10 24; www.bellevue.it; Hotel Bellevue Syrene, Piazza della Vittoria 5)

Syrenuse Bar

BAR

22 MAP P132, E4

Hogging Piazza Tasso's busiest spot, the Syrenuse is where locals pile in before, during or after the evening *passeggiata* (stroll) for a piazza-side *aperitivo* (pre-dinner drink). Drinks are reasonably priced (for Sorrento) and the complimentary bites – such as *pizzette* and *zeppole* (savoury doughnuts) – are a step up from the stock-standard nuts and chips. There's regular live music on Saturday night. (081 807 55 82; www.barsyrenusesorrento.it; Piazza Tasso; 7.30am-late;)

Cafè Latino

BAR

23 MAP P132, C5

Think locked-eyes-over-cocktails time. This is the place to impress your date with cocktails (from €7) on the terrace, surrounded by orange and lemon trees. Sip a Mary Pickford (rum, pineapple, *grenadino* and maraschino) or a glass of chilled white wine. If you can't drag yourselves away, you can also eat here (meals around €35). (081 877 37 18; www.cafelatinosorrento.it; Vico Fuoro 4a; 10am-1am Mar-Dec)

Shopping

Bottega 21

FASHION & ACCESSORIES

24 MAP P132, D4

This is the Sorrento branch of Neapolitan leather workshop Bottega 21, known for its stylish, handcrafted leather goods. Shop for fetching totes, handbags, duffel bags and backpacks, nifty tobacco pouches, wallets, coin purses and unisex belts. The workshop only uses high-quality Tuscan leather, offered in natural, earthy hues and bolder block colours. (081 807 35 85; www.bottegaventuno.it; Via Torquato Tasso 19; 10am-2pm & 4-10pm Tue & Wed, 10am-2pm & 2.30-10pm Thu-Mon summer, reduced hours rest of year, closed Jan–mid-Mar)

The SITA Bus Experience

Thanks to its precipitous topography, the Amalfi Coast never benefited from a railway line. Instead, modern train passengers offloaded in Sorrento in the west or Salerno in the east must take their lives into their own hands and hire a car, or put their lives into someone else's hands and hop onto one of the region's blue SITA buses.

The spectacular road you'll be driving along is called Strada Statale 163, aka the Nastro Azzurro (Blue Ribbon). It wends its way along the Amalfi Coast between Vietri sul Mare and Sant'Agata sui due Golfi, near Sorrento, snaking round impossibly tight curves, over deep ravines and through tunnels gouged out of sheer rock.

Which is where the skill of your bus driver comes in. You haven't really experienced the Amalfi Coast until you've sat through the theatre of a SITA bus ride, squeezing past lines of cars where motorists exchange hand gestures, or screeching around hairpin bends where waist-high barriers are all that exist between you and oblivion. With a liberal use of their loud klaxons, bus drivers seem to take the latent dangers in their stride, sitting at their wheels like Formula One racing drivers blessed with super-human peripheral vision.

SITA buses stop at numerous places along the coast with Amalfi town acting as the main nexus. Buy a ticket in a tobacconist shop or a bar, validate it as you climb on board, and enjoy the ride. Popular bus routes get crowded in July and August, so be prepared to stand.

Stinga — ARTS & CRAFTS

25 MAP P132, E4

Well worth seeking out, this place sells distinctive inlaid-wood items made in Sorrento by the same family of craftspeople for three generations. The pieces are highly original, especially in their use of colour and design, which is often mosaic or geometric. Fine jewellery made by family member Amulè, including coral pieces, is also on display. (081 878 11 30; www.stingatarsia.com; Via Luigi de Maio 16; 9am-8.30pm)

Terrerosse — CERAMICS

26 MAP P132, C4

Inspired by local marine life, history and mythology, Alessandro Ottone and his partner Enrica Cerchia create some of Sorrento's most idiosyncratic ceramics. Fish pop out of plates, and surfaces are often etched with whimsical patterns. You'll find everything from platters and coffee cups to lamps and jewellery. Crockery products are non-toxic and dishwasher safe. (349 7542872, 081 807 32 77; Via Fuoro 73; 10am-10pm Apr-Oct, 10am-1.30pm & 3.30-7pm Nov-Mar)

Survival Guide

Toledo Metro Station (p60), Naples

Before You Go

Book Your Stay

- In Naples, the lively *centro storico* (historic centre) is home to most of the city's cultural and historical sights. Seafront Santa Lucia delivers grand hotels, while Chiaia is best for fashionable boutiques and trendy bars. The earthy Quartieri Spagnoli is within walking distance of all three neighbourhoods.
- Accommodation on the islands, Amalfi Coast and in Sorrento tends towards the higher end of the market and is generally seasonal. Options run the gamut from historic *palazzi* (mansions) to idiosyncratic B&Bs, with a sprinkling of budget *pensioni* and campsites.
- The high season is July and August, though prices peak again around Easter and Christmas. Book in advance during these periods. Conversely, prices drop between 30% and 50% in low season.

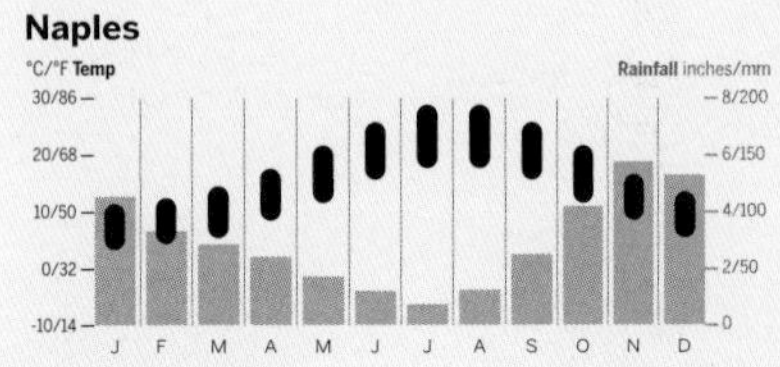

When to Go

Winter (Dec–Feb) Cold, wet days. Museums are quiet and prices are low except at Christmas and New Year. Many coastal hotels and restaurants are shut.

Spring (Mar–May) Lively Easter celebrations and cultural festivals. May sometimes delivers summer-like warmth.

Summer (Jun–Aug) Hot days, with peak accommodation rates, crowds and activities on the islands and Amalfi Coast. Many restaurants and shops in Naples close for a few weeks in August.

Autumn (Sep–Nov) September generally delivers summer heat without the August crowds and traffic.

Useful Websites

Halldis (www.halldis.com) Offers short- and longer-term apartments across the city.

Lonely Planet (www.lonelyplanet.com/italy/campania/naples/hotels) Trusted recommendations.

Best Budget

The Church (www.thechurch.it) Upcycled art and furniture in a history-packed *centro storico palazzo*.

Magma Home (www.magmahome.it) B&B with salvaged architectural details, intriguing art and knockout rooftop terraces.

Schiara (www.maisonsdecharme.it) Contemporary takes on southern themes and a killer rooftop terrace in the *centro storico*.

B&B Arte e Musei (www.facebook.com/bnbarteemusei) Three sparkling rooms decorated by a hospitable artist owner.

Best Midrange

La Ciliegina Lifestyle Hotel (www.ciliegina hotel.it) White-on-white chic and a rooftop Jacuzzi by Via Toledo.

Hotel Piazza Bellini (www.hotelpiazza bellini.com) Contemporary lodgings in a 16th-century *palazzo* by Piazza Bellini.

Casa D'Anna (www.casadanna.it) A plush, Gallic-accented hideaway in the heart of La Sanità.

Atelier Inès (www.atelierinesgallery.com) Unique, detail-focused rooms adorned with collectible Neapolitan artworks in La Sanità.

Best Top End

Grand Hotel Vesuvio (www.vesuvio.it) The grand duke of Naples' seafront hotels.

Eurostars Hotel Excelsior (www.euro starshotels.it) Fin-de-siècle glamour overlooking Naples' bay and volcano.

Grand Hotel Parker's (www.grandhotel parkers.com) Illustrious hillside *palazzo* with smashing views and a lauded in-house spa.

Romeo Hotel (www.romeohotel.it) Contemporary, port-side digs with high-tech gadgetry and rooftop pool.

Arriving in Naples

Naples International Airport (Capodichino)

Naples International Airport (Capodichino) (☎081 789 62 59; www.aeroportodinapoli.it; Viale F Ruffo di Calabria), 7km northeast of the city centre, is southern Italy's main airport. It's served by a number of major airlines and low-cost carriers, including easyJet, which operates flights to Naples from London, Paris, Amsterdam, Vienna, Berlin and several other European cities.

Bus (☎800 639525; www.anm.it; €5) The Alibus airport shuttle connects the airport to Napoli Centrale (Piazza Garibaldi) and the Molo Angioino cruise-ship terminal, located beside the Molo Beverello fast-ferry and hydrofoil terminal. One-way tickets cost €5 and can be purchased on board. Buses run every 10 to 30 minutes.

Taxi Official taxi fares from the airport are as follows: €25 to Chiaia, Mergellina and Posillipo; €21 to Piazza Municipio or the Molo Beverello fast-ferry and hydrofoil terminal; and €18 to Napoli Centrale (Piazza Garibaldi) and the *centro storico*. Taxi companies include **Consortaxi** (☎081 22 22; www.consortaxi.com), **Radio Taxi La Partenope** (☎081 01 01; www.radiotaxilapartenope.it) and **Taxi Napoli** (☎081 88 88; www.taxinapoli.it).

Napoli Centrale

Naples is southern Italy's rail hub and on the main Milan–Palermo line, with good connections to other Italian cities and towns.

The city's main train station is **Napoli Centrale** (Stazione Centrale; ☎081 554 31 88; Piazza Garibaldi), just east of the *centro storico*. From here, the national rail company **Trenitalia** (☎892021; www.trenitalia.com)

runs regular direct services to Rome (2nd class €12 to €48, 70 minutes to three hours, around 66 daily). High-speed private rail company **Italo** (☎892020; www.italotreno.it) also runs daily direct services to Rome (2nd class €15 to €39, 70 minutes, around 20 daily). Most Italo services stop at Roma Termini and Roma Tiburtina stations.

Metropark Napoli Centrale

Long-distance domestic and international buses arrive at **Metropark Napoli Centrale** (☎800 65 00 06; Corso Arnaldo Lucci; Ⓜ Garibaldi), which flanks the southern end of Napoli Centrale train station.

Molo Angioino & Calata Porta di Massa

Slow ferries for Sicily, the Aeolian Islands and Sardinia sail from **Molo Angioino** (right beside Molo Beverello) and neighbouring **Calata Porta di Massa**. Car ferries to Ischia and Procida also depart from Calata Porta di Massa. Both terminals are within walking distance of Municipio metro station on Line 1, which reaches Napoli Centrale (Garibaldi), the city's main train station.

Getting Around

Metro

Line 1

- Like city buses, **Metro Line 1** (Linea 1; www.anm.it) is operated by **ANM** (☎800 639525; www.anm.it).
- Trains run from Garibaldi (Napoli Centrale) to Vomero and the northern suburbs via the city centre.
- Useful stops include Duomo and Università (southern edge of the *centro storico*), Municipio (hydrofoil and ferry terminals), Toledo (Via Toledo and Quartieri Spagnoli), Dante (western edge of the *centro storico*) and Museo Archeologico Nazionale).

Line 2

- **Metro Line 2** (Linea 2; www.trenitalia.com/tcom/Treni-Regionali/Campania) is operated by Italy's state-owned Ferrovie dello Stato (FS).
- Trains runs from Gianturco to Garibaldi (Napoli Centrale) and on to Pozzuoli.
- Useful stops include Piazza Cavour (La Sanità and northern edge of *centro storico*), Piazza Amedeo (Chiaia) and Mergellina (Mergellina ferry and hydrofoil terminal). Change for Line 1 at Garibaldi or Piazza Cavour (known as Museo on Line 1).

Bus

- ANM operates city buses in Naples.
- Purchase your ticket at kiosks, tobacconists and vending machines and validate it in the validation machines on the bus.
- There is no central station for city buses, but most pass through Piazza Garibaldi.
- Some city bus routes do not run on Sunday.
- A small number of routes run through the

night, marked with an 'N' before their route number.

Funicular

All four funicular lines in Naples are run by **ANM** (www.anm.it; 7am-10pm).

Funicolare Centrale Travels from Piazzetta Augusteo to Piazza Fuga.

Funicolare di Chiaia Travels from Via del Parco Margherita to Via Domenico Cimarosa.

Funicolare di Montesanto Travels from Piazza Montesanto to Via Raffaele Morghen.

Funicolare di Mergellina Connects the waterfront at Via Mergellina with Via Manzoni.

Taxi

- Official taxis are white and metered. Always ensure the meter is running.
- The minimum starting fare is €3.50 (€6.50 on Sunday), with a baffling range of additional charges, all of which are listed at www.taxinapoli.it/tariffe. These extras include the following: €1.50 for a radio taxi call, €4 for an airport run, €5 for trips starting at the airport and €0.50 per piece of luggage in the boot (trunk).
- Guide dogs and wheelchairs are carried free of charge.
- There are taxi stands located at most of the city's main piazzas. Book a taxi by calling **Consortaxi** (081 22 22; www.consortaxi.com), **Taxi Napoli** (081 88 88; www.taxinapoli.it) or **Radio Taxi La Partenope** (081 01 01; www.radiotaxilapartenope.it).

Boat

- Naples, the bay islands and the Amalfi Coast are served by a comprehensive ferry network.
- Catch fast ferries and hydrofoils for Capri, Sorrento, Ischia (both

Tickets

- **TIC** (Ticket Integrato Campani) tickets – available at kiosks, tobacconists and vending machines – are valid on all city metro, bus, and funicular services, including **Circumvesuviana** (800 211388; www.eavsrl.it) and **Cumana** (800 21 13 88; www.eavsrl.it) trains within the Naples city zone.
- The TIC *biglietto integrato urbano* (€1.60 for 90 minutes) allows for only one trip on each mode of transport (except buses) within 90 minutes of validation.
- The TIC *biglietto giornaliero integrato urbano* (€4.50, daily), valid until midnight from validation, allows for unlimited travel on all city buses, metro trains and funiculars.
- The city's various transport companies offer their own tickets, for use on their services only. For example, **ANM** (800 639525; www.anm.it) – which runs city buses, the four funiculars, and metro lines 1 and 6 – offers a €1.10 single-use ticket. State railway company **Ferrovie dello Stato (FS)** runs metro line 2, offering a €1.30 single-use ticket for use on that metro line.

Ischia Porto and Forio) and Procida from Molo Beverello in front of Castel Nuovo.

- Hydrofoils for Capri, Ischia and Procida also sail from Mergellina.

Car & Motorcycle

- Much of central Naples is off-limits to non-resident vehicles, and the anarchic traffic and illegal parking attendants demanding tips will quickly ruin your holiday.
- Nonresident vehicles are prohibited on Capri for much of the year, and driving is largely discouraged on Ischia and Procida.
- Peak-season traffic can make driving along the Amalfi Coast stressful, though having your own vehicle here means ultimate flexibility.

Essential Information

Accessible Travel

- Cobbled streets, hair-raising traffic, blocked pavements and narrow lifts (or a complete lack of them) make life difficult for travellers with limited mobility, sight or hearing.
- Some efforts are being made to make Naples more accessible. Wheelchair-friendly ramps, lifts and toilets are common at museums and train stations, and while many restaurants are not yet completely wheelchair-friendly, most will try to accommodate guests with disabilities (consider calling ahead).
- Some city buses have extra-large central doors, access ramps and dedicated space for a wheelchair; these are marked with a wheelchair symbol.
- Numerous hydrofoils and ferries are also wheelchair-friendly; reserve your ticket in advance to ensure that your vessel is compatible.
- Some taxis are equipped to carry passengers in wheelchairs; ask for a taxi for a *sedia a rotelle* (wheelchair).
- Italy's national rail company, **Trenitalia** (☎892021; www.trenitalia.com) offers a national helpline for passengers with a disability at ☎199 303060 (6.45am to 9.30pm daily). To secure assistance at **Napoli Centrale** (Stazione Centrale; ☎081 554 31 88; Piazza Garibaldi), you should call this number 24 hours prior to your departure.

Business Hours

Opening hours will often vary between individual businesses and/or branches.

Banks 8.30am–1.30pm and 2.45–3.45pm or 4.15pm Monday to Friday

Restaurants 12.30–3pm and 7.30–11pm or midnight

Cafes 7.30am–8pm

Clubs 11pm–5am

Shops 9am–1pm and 3.30–7.30pm (or 4–8pm) Monday to Saturday, some close Monday morning and some open Sunday

Discount Cards

- If you're planning to blitz the sights, the **Campania Artecard** (☎800 600601; www.campaniartecard.it) is an excellent investment.
- The Naples three-day ticket (adult/reduced €21/12) gives free admission to three

participating sites, up to 50% off on others and free use of public transport in the city.

- The seven-day 'Tutta la Regione' ticket (€34) offers free admission to five sites and discounted admission to others in areas as far afield as Caserta and Ravello (Amalfi Coast). This version does not cover transport.
- Cards can be purchased online or at sites.

Electricity

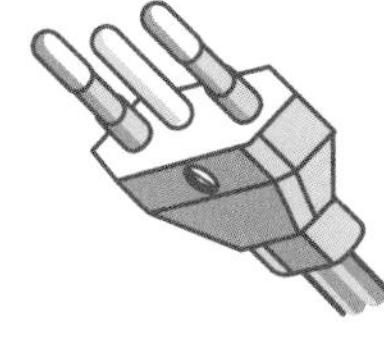

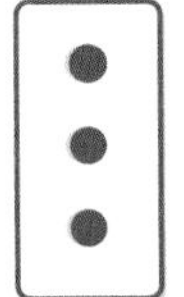

Type L
230V/50Hz

Emergency

Ambulance ☎ 118

Police ☎ 112/113

Fire ☎ 115

LGBTIQ+ Travellers

- While homosexuality is generally well tolerated in Naples (especially among younger generations), many gay Neapolitans remain in the closet (at least partially) and overt displays of affection by same-sex couples can still attract stares or comments. Discretion is advisable.
- Areas known as popular gay haunts include **Piazza Bellini** (Ⓜ Dante) in the *centro storico*.
- Useful online resources include **Arcigay Napoli** (www.arcigaynapoli.org, in Italian), **Napoli Gay Press** (www.napoligaypress.it, in Italian) and **Gay-Friendly Italy** (www.gayfriendlyitaly.com, in English).

Money

ATMs & Credit Cards

- Bancomats (ATMs) are widely available and the best way to obtain local currency.
- International credit and debit cards can be used in any Bancomat displaying the appropriate sign. Cards are also good for payment in most hotels, restaurants, shops and supermarkets.
- Check any charges with your bank. Most banks now build a fee of around 3% into every foreign transaction. In addition, ATM withdrawals can attract a further fee, usually around 1.5%.

Tipping

Neapolitans are not big tippers, but the following is a guide:

Taxis Round up to the nearest euro.

Hotels Tip porters about €5 at high-end hotels.

Restaurants If *servizio* (service) is not included on your bill, leave a euro or two in pizzerias, or 10% of the bill in restaurants.

Bars Neapolitans usually place a €0.10 coin on the bar when ordering their coffee; if drinks are brought to your table, a small tip is generally appreciated.

Public Holidays

New Year's Day (Capodanno) 1 January

Epiphany (Epifania) 6 January

Dos & Donts

Italy is a surprisingly formal society; the following tips will help you avoid any awkward moments.

Greetings Shake hands and say *buongiorno* (good day) or *buonasera* (good evening) to strangers; kiss both cheeks and say *come stai?* (how are you?) for friends. Use *Lei* (you) in polite company; use *tu* (you) with friends and children. Only use first names if invited.

Gestures Maintain eye contact during conversation and when toasting.

Asking for help Say *mi scusi* (excuse me) to attract attention; use *permesso* (permission) when you want to pass by in a crowded space.

Eating and drinking When dining in an Italian home, bring wine or a small gift of *dolci* (sweets) from a local *pasticceria*. Let your host lead when sitting and starting the meal.

Visiting churches It is considered disrespectful to visit churches as a tourist during Mass and other worship services. Taking photos at such times is especially frowned upon.

Visiting archaeological sites Refrain from touching frescoes and never use a flash when photographing them.

Easter Monday (Pasquetta) March/April

Liberation Day (Giorno della Liberazione) 25 April

Labour Day (Festa del Lavoro) 1 May

Republic Day (Festa della Repubblica) 2 June

Feast of the Assumption (Assunzione or Ferragosto) 15 August

All Saints' Day (Ognisanti) 1 November

Feast of the Immaculate Conception (Festa della Immacolata Concezione) 8 December

Christmas Day (Natale) 25 December

Boxing Day (Festa di Santo Stefano) 26 December

Responsible Travel

- Hit the Amalfi coast in the shoulder season months of April and October and stay on the quieter eastern shoreline.
- Seek out restaurants affiliated with the Slow Food movement that plug traditional regional products.
- Use buses and trains rather than hiring a car. The Amalfi coast is well served with SITA buses. The Circumvesuviana train runs between Naples and Sorrento.
- Stay in an agriturismo. These government regulated farmstays push sustainable practices and home-grown food. There's a smattering of them along the Amalfi coast and on the Sorrento Peninsula.

Safe Travel

Despite its reputation, Naples is a relatively

safe place, especially if you heed the following basic safety tips:

- Avoid keeping money, credit cards and other valuables in easy-to-reach pockets as pickpockets do operate on crowded metro trains, buses and at markets.
- Never leave your bags unattended. At cafes and bars, loop your bag's strap around your leg while seated.
- Although scooter-riding petty thieves are a much rarer phenomenon these days, it doesn't hurt to wear bags and cameras across your body, away from the street.
- At archaeological sites, watch out for touts posing as legitimate guides.

Telephone

- Italy's country code is ☎39 and the Naples area code is ☎081.

Mobile Phones

- Italian mobile phones operate on the GSM 900/1800 network, compatible with the rest of Europe and Australia but not always with the North American systems.
- The cheapest way of using your mobile is to buy a *prepagato* (prepaid) Italian SIM card.

Toilets

Beyond museums, department stores and train stations, there are few public toilets in Naples. If you're caught short, the best thing to do is to nip into a cafe or bar. The polite thing to do is to order something at the bar. You may need to pay to use public toilets at some venues (usually €0.50 to €1).

Tourist Information

Tourist Information Office (Map p36; ☎081 551 27 01; www.inaples.it; Piazza del Gesù Nuovo 7; 🕒9am-5pm Mon-Sat, to 1pm Sun; Ⓜ Dante) In the *centro storico*.

Tourist Information Office (Map p58; ☎081 40 23 94; www.inaples.it; Via San Carlo 9; 🕒9am-5pm Mon-Sat, to 1pm Sun; 🚌R2 to Via San Carlo, Ⓜ Municipio) At Galleria Umberto I, directly opposite Teatro San Carlo.

Visas

- Italy is one of the 26 European countries to make up the Schengen area.
- EU citizens do not need a visa to enter Italy – an identification card or passport is sufficient.
- Nationals of Australia, Canada, Israel, Japan, New Zealand, Switzerland and the USA do not need a visa if they are staying in Italy up to 90 days.
- Nationals of other countries will need to obtain a Schengen tourist visa – to check the requirements for a Schengen visa, visit www.schengenvisainfo.com/tourist-schengen-visa.

Language

Standard Italian is taught and spoken throughout Italy. Regional dialects are an important part of identity in many parts of the country, but you'll have no trouble being understood anywhere if you stick to standard Italian, which we've also used in this chapter.

The sounds used in spoken Italian can all be found in English. If you read our pronunciation guides as if they were English, you'll be understood. The stressed syllables are indicated with italics. Note that *ai* is pronounced as in 'aisle', *ay* as in 'say', *ow* as in 'how', *dz* as the 'ds' in 'lids', and that *r* is a strong, rolled sound.

To enhance your trip with a phrasebook, visit lonelyplanet.com.

Basics

Hello.
Buongiorno. bwon·*jor*·no

Goodbye.
Arrivederci. a·ree·ve·*der*·chee

How are you?
Come sta? *ko*·me sta

Fine. And you?
Bene. E Lei? *be*·ne e lay

Please.
Per favore. per fa·*vo*·re

Thank you.
Grazie. *gra*·tsye

Excuse me.
Mi scusi. mee *skoo*·zee

Sorry.
Mi dispiace. mee dees·*pya*·che

Yes./No.
Sì./No. see/no

I don't understand.
Non capisco. non ka·*pee*·sko

Do you speak English?
Parla inglese? *par*·la een·*gle*·ze

Eating & Drinking

I'd like ...	*Vorrei ...*	vo·*ray* ..
a coffee	*un caffè*	oon ka·*fe*
a table	*un tavolo*	oon *ta*·vo·lo
the menu	*il menù*	eel me·*noo*
two beers	*due birre*	doo·e *bee*·re

What would you recommend?
Cosa mi consiglia? ko·za mee kon·*see*·lya

Enjoy the meal!
Buon appetito! bwon a·pe·*tee*·to

That was delicious!
Era squisito! e·ra skwee·zee·to

Cheers!
Salute! sa·*loo*·te

Please bring the bill.
Mi porta il conto, per favore? mee *por*·ta eel *kon* to per fa·*vo*·re

Shopping

I'd like to buy ...
Vorrei comprare ... vo·*ray* kom·*pra*·re ...

I'm just looking.
Sto solo guardando. sto *so*·lo gwar·*dan*·do

How much is this?

Quanto costa questo?	*kwan*·to *kos*·ta *kwe*·sto

It's too expensive.

È troppo caro/ cara. (m/f)	e *tro*·po *ka*·ro/ *ka*·ra

Emergencies

Help!

Aiuto!	a·*yoo*·to

Call the police!

Chiami la polizia!	*kya*·mee la po·lee·*tsee*·a

Call a doctor!

Chiami un medico!	*kya*·mee oon *me*·dee·ko

I'm sick.

Mi sento male.	mee *sen*·to *ma*·le

I'm lost.

Mi sono perso/ persa. (m/f)	mee so·no *per*·so/ *per*·sa

Where are the toilets?

Dove sono i gabinetti?	*do*·ve so·no ee ga·bee·*ne*·tee

Time & Numbers

What time is it?

Che ora è?	ke *o*·ra e

It's (two) o'clock.

Sono le (due).	*so*·no le (*doo*·e)

morning	*mattina*	ma·*tee*·na
afternoon	*pomeriggio*	po·me·*ree*·jo
evening	*sera*	*se*·ra
yesterday	*ieri*	*ye*·ree
today	*oggi*	*o*·jee
tomorrow	*domani*	do·*ma*·nee

1	*uno*	*oo*·no
2	*due*	*doo*·e
3	*tre*	*tre*
4	*quattro*	*kwa*·tro
5	*cinque*	*cheen*·kwe
6	*sei*	say
7	*sette*	*se*·te
8	*otto*	*o*·to
9	*nove*	*no*·ve
10	*dieci*	*dye*·chee
100	*cento*	*chen*·to
1000	*mille*	*mee*·le

Transport & Directions

Where's ...?

Dov'è ...?	do·*ve* ...

What's the address?

Qual'è l'indirizzo?	kwa·*le* leen·dee·*ree*·tso

Can you show me (on the map)?

Può mostrarmi (sulla pianta)?	pwo mos·*trar*·mee (soo·la *pyan*·ta)

At what time does the ... leave?

A che ora parte ...?	a ke *o*·ra *par*·te

Does it stop at ...?

Si ferma a ...?	see *fer*·ma a ...

How do I get there?

Come ci si arriva?	*ko*·me chee see a·*ree*·va

bus	*l'autobus*	*low*·to·boos
ticket	*un biglietto*	oon bee·*lye*·to
timetable	*orario*	o·*ra*·ryo
train	*il treno*	eel *tre*·no

Behind the Scenes

Send Us Your Feedback

We love to hear from travellers – your comments help make our books better. We read every word, and we guarantee that your feedback goes straight to the authors. Visit **lonelyplanet.com/contact** to submit your updates and suggestions.

Note: We may edit, reproduce and incorporate your comments in Lonely Planet products such as guidebooks, websites and digital products, so let us know if you don't want your comments reproduced or your name acknowledged. For a copy of our privacy policy visit lonelyplanet.com/privacy.

Acknowledgements

Cover photographs: (front) Pizza, Naples, Olga_Go/Shutterstock ©; (back) Villa Rufolo, Ravello, Gaspar Janos/Shutterstock ©

Photographs pp24–5 (clockwise from top right): Alex DeG/Shutterstock©, Giannis Papanikos/Shutterstock©, Javen/Shutterstock©, S-F/Shutterstock©, Greg Elms/Lonely Planet©, Giambattista Lazazzera/Shutterstock ©

Cristian's Thanks

Grazie infinite to my *'Re e Regina di Napoli',* Federica Rispoli and Ivan Palmieri, Igor Milanese, Gabriella De Micco, Valentina Vellusi, Mirella Armiero, Andrea Maglio, Susy Galeone, Enzo Porzio, Marcello De Bossa, Luca Coda, Harriet Driver, Alfredo Cefalo, Malgorzata Gajo, as well as the many other generous Neapolitans who kindly shared their city insights and secrets. At Lonely Planet, a big thank you to Anna Tyler for the commission and to my co-writer Brendan Sainsbury for his stellar research.

Brendan's Thanks

Molte grazie to all the skilled Sita bus drivers, helpful tourist information staff, generous B&B owners, expert pizza kneaders, and innocent passers-by who helped me, unwittingly or otherwise, during my research trip. Special thanks to Alfonso and Rosalia in Agropoli for their help in the Cilento region. Thanks also to my wife, Elizabeth; my son, Kieran; and my sister, Theresa for their company on the road.

This Book

This 2nd edition of Lonely Planet's *Pocket Naples & the Amalfi Coast* guidebook was researched and written by Cristian Bonetto and Brendan Sainsbury. Cristian and Brendan also wrote the 1st edition. This guidebook was produced by the following:

Senior Product Editors Amy Lynch, Elizabeth Jones

Product Editors Katie Connolly, Alison Ridgway

Senior Cartographers Anthony Phelan, Julie Sheridan

Book Designers Catalina Aragón, Clara Monitto, Mazzy Prinsep

Assisting Editors Will Allen, Alex Conroy, Lucie Cowie, Barbara Delissen, Andrea Dobbin, Emma Gibbs, Jodie Martire, Gabrielle Stefanos

Cover Researcher Brendan Dempsey-Spencer

Thanks to Imogen Bannister, Sonia Kapoor, Claire Naylor, Darren O'Connell, Martine Power

Index

See also separate subindexes for:

Eating p159
Drinking p159
Entertainment p159
Shopping p159

Sights 000
Map Pages **000**

Sights 000
Map Pages **000**

Our Writers

Cristian Bonetto

Cristian has contributed to more than 30 Lonely Planet guides to date, including *New York City*, *Italy*, *Venice & the Veneto*, *Naples & the Amalfi Coast*, *Denmark*, *Copenhagen*, *Sweden* and *Singapore*. Lonely Planet work aside, his musings on travel, food, culture and design appear in numerous publications around the world, including *The Telegraph* (UK) and *Corriere del Mezzogiorno* (Italy). When not on the road, you'll find the reformed playwright and TV scriptwriter slurping espresso in his beloved hometown, Melbourne.

Brendan Sainsbury

Born and raised in the UK in a town that never merits a mention in any guidebook (Andover, Hampshire), Brendan spent the holidays of his youth caravanning in the English Lake District and didn't leave Blighty until he was 19. Making up for lost time, he's since squeezed 70 countries into a sometimes precarious existence as a writer and professional vagabond. In the last 11 years, he has written more than 40 books for Lonely Planet about places ranging from from Castro's Cuba to the canyons of Peru.

Published by Lonely Planet Global Limited
CRN 554153
2nd edition – Jun 2022
ISBN 978 1 78868 420 0

10 9 8 7 6 5 4 3 2 1
Printed in Malaysia

Eating

Drinking

Entertainment

Shopping